Lessons from the Learner

Student-generated activities for the language classroom

Pilgrims

Sheelagh Deller

Longman

Longman Group UK Limited,
Longman House, Burnt Mill, Harlow,
Essex CM20 2JE, England
and Associated Companies throughout the world.

© Longman Group UK Limited 1990

This book is produced in association
with Pilgrims Language Courses Limited
of Canterbury, England.

First published 1990

Set in Linotron 10/12pt Cheltenham

Printed in Great Britain
by Richard Clay plc, Bungay, Suffolk

British Library Cataloguing in Publication Data
Deller, Sheelagh
Lessons from the learner: student generated activities
for the language classroom. — (Pilgrims Longman
teachers resource book)
1. Non-English speaking students. Curriculum subjects:
English language. Teaching
I. Title
420.2407

ISBN 0 582 07004 X

Acknowledgements
The author and publisher thank Brian Abbs, Ingrid
Freebairn and Longman Group UK Ltd for granting
permission to use pages 60 to 67 of *Opening Strategies*
(Longman 1982).

Illustrations
Cover illustrated by Ken Cox

A letter from the Series Editors

Dear Teacher,

This series of teachers' resource books has developed from Pilgrims' involvement in running courses for learners of English and for teachers and teacher trainers.

Our aim is to pass on ideas, techniques and practical activities which we know work in the classroom. Our authors, both Pilgrims' teachers and like-minded colleagues in other organisations, present accounts of innovative procedures which will broaden the range of options available to teachers working within communicative and humanistic approaches.

We would be very interested to receive your impressions of the series. If you notice any omissions that we ought to record in future editions, or if you think of any interesting variations, please let us know. We will be glad to acknowledge all contributions that we are able to use.

Seth Lindstromberg
Series Editor

Mario Rinvolucri
Series Consultant

Pilgrims Language Courses
Canterbury
Kent
CT1 3HG
England

Acknowledgements

Mario Rinvolucri for all I have learnt from him, for giving me the confidence to write this book, and for so much constructive support in the hilly process.

Roger Woodham for giving me the opportunity to work in Poland.

The teachers in Poland who forced me to focus on the problems of not enough materials, books or time.

Simon Greenall for his constant support and also for my start-of-the-day tape.

Seth Lindstromberg for his calm sanity and sound advice.

Teresa Doguelli for being Teresa Doguelli.

Flight BA 731 2.12.88. from Geneva for being 3 hours late and inspiring me for the introduction to this book.

Wojtek Krajewski for being on flight BA 731, and for starting me off in the world of EFL.

My sons for laughing at me.

Sheelagh Deller
Canterbury
August 1989

Sheelagh Deller

Sheelagh Deller is a freelance language teacher and teacher trainer. She lives in Canterbury and has had strong ties with Pilgrims since 1980. She is very much a classroom practitioner and divides her time fairly evenly between language teaching and teacher training. A lot of her work is with the British Council, running teacher training seminars in and out of Britain. She has travelled extensively in Europe and North Africa, working with teachers covering wide ranges of experience, culture and teaching situations. She has three sons.

Contents

Index of activities

Who is this book for?

- Language teachers of any language.

- Experienced teachers who feel they might be stagnating and want another strategy.

- Inexperienced teachers who want ideas which provide their students with opportunities to use and practise the language.

- Teachers of ESP and General Business courses.

- Teachers of one-to-one, small classes or large classes.

- Teachers of mono or multi-lingual classes.

- Teachers of mono or multi-level classes.

- Teacher trainers working in countries where teachers have not enough materials, books or preparation time.

- Teachers of secondary school children.

Appetiser

FILING

When I started teaching, I used to hoard materials such as newspapers, articles, magazines, pictures and poems, misguidedly thinking that one rainy day I would go through them to see if there was anything there I could use in my teaching. Of course I never did, as it takes far too long, and I could never face it. Now I still keep these things but I give them to my students to sort out. They sometimes do this in groups in the classroom, or at other times for homework.

The tasks can vary. Here are some possibilities:
1 Find something you think the rest of the group would like to read and be prepared to introduce it, ask questions about it, or explain it.
2 Find something with a lot of examples of the past tense and prepare a cloze exercise.
3 Classify materials that you like into different topics.
4 Classify materials that you like into different grammatical areas.
5 Classify materials that you like into different styles of language.
6 Grade the materials you like from very difficult to very easy.

Learners feel happy to use materials they have found for the purpose they have chosen, so there is a good chance of high motivation and commitment to the work that follows on. If you would like more information about the rationale behind this and the other activities in the book you will find it in the Introduction that follows.

Introduction

THE POWER OF THE LEARNER

I am writing this at Heathrow Airport Terminal 1 waiting to meet a plane that is three hours late. There are a number of situations that haunt me; namely waiting at airports, being in prison, being in a traffic jam on the M25, and being a learner in a classroom situation. Being, being, being. All in the present and extremely continuous. The common factor which most affects me in these situations is my total lack of control or choice. I feel helpless and frustrated, so much so that I temporarily lose my sense of identity and responsibility. And the worst thing is that there is no tangible target for my frustration.

So one objective of this book is how to avoid these feelings arising in the classroom, in other words, how to create more situations in which the learners can contribute, initiate, control, and create what happens in the classroom. I use the word 'more' advisedly as I don't pretend that everything we do in the classroom should focus on this.

THE FEELINGS OF THE TEACHER

On the other hand, this book is certainly not intended to benefit only the learners. As a teacher I am just as interested in and concerned about how we as teachers feel, whether we be new, inexperienced teachers or experienced and perhaps jaded ones. There is a lot of thought, work and time given to teacher development these days. This is very important. However, I am equally concerned about how to stop ourselves as teachers actually going backwards. For teachers in this situation (and I have met many of them, including myself) there is less support or sympathy. If we are new to the job and naturally enthusiastic, there are plenty of opportunities to develop and learn. But our unsung trainers are our learners. They are the really powerful influence on our 'on the job' development. If we have been teaching the same syllabus with the same books in the same classrooms for a number of years, it may be difficult to sustain much enthusiasm, interest, creativity or spark. An analogy of this for me is my time as a non-working(?!) mother of three small boys. Meals were my problem. Not so much cooking them but being able to enjoy eating them. There was no element of surprise. My biggest treat was to eat in someone else's house where I had no idea what to expect. In the same way, if everything that happens in the classroom has originated from us, then we are not in for many surprises. If we always decide on and devise the activities, topics, materials etc. to be used, we inevitably lose the element of surprise. On the other hand, if there are times when we can't predict the material, we give ourselves the opportunity to think on our feet, experiment, be stimulated by our learners and experience new ideas and situations.

A SOLUTION

So there are two objectives in this book: one for the learners and another for ourselves. One way of achieving both of these is for us as teachers to set up activities where the learners generate the material and then use it for other linguistic activities. Put simply, if we want our learners to focus on the past tense, they could do this using material they have previously produced themselves. In practice this often means a reversal of the usual process, i.e. starting with the freer activities which are then used for more controlled practice. For example, the learners can create such things as jumbled stories, cloze exercises and transformation exercises for each other, from material they have previously produced themselves. This material has the advantage of being understood by them, feeling close to them, and perhaps most importantly of all, being *theirs* rather than something imposed on them. As a result they feel more comfortable and involved, and have no problems in identifying with it.

This book focuses on different ways of generating these student materials, with some suggestions, where appropriate, on how they could be exploited for further language practice.

THE BACKGROUND TO THIS APPROACH

I have developed this approach as a direct result of three important influences:
1 Community Language Learning. This approach uses language which is generated and recorded by the students as the material for working on grammar, pronunciation and vocabulary. The material is generated by the students asking in their mother tongue for a translation of the language they want to say in the target language. When they feel confident enough they record it. In this book I am suggesting other ways of initially generating this material. For further reading about Community Language Learning see *Counselling Learning* (Curran 1972) and *Teaching Languages: A Way and a Ways* (Stevick 1980).
2 My work as a teacher of ESP and Business English where I have often been in a situation where my students know much more about the 'subject matter' than I do, e.g. marketing, banking, chemistry, medicine. In such situations the students can generate relevant material which we can then use for specific language practice.
3 My work with teachers who have large classes, low-tech materials, inadequate books, and little preparation time.

THE ACTIVITIES

Each activity is introduced with information about the level, time, materials and numbers.

1 **Levels** I have indicated the lowest possible level, but in all cases the activity can be used at higher levels, and usually with mixed levels – because students will do the activity at their own level.

2 **Times** These do not include the time taken for the possible follow-on activites, even though suggestions for these are often included. Some activities are time-consuming, but the time is well spent as they involve a variety of language skills, i.e. one of these activities could be covering the same amount of language practice as a unit of a coursebook. Also, there are often stages which could be done as homework.

3 **Materials** Very few of the activities require special materials. I have assumed the students each have a pen and paper, and that there is a white or blackboard in the classroom.

4 **Numbers** Activities can often be adapted to suit different numbers of students. For activities marked 'minimum two' the teaching can be one of the pair in one-to-one teaching. Most activities are done in groups so work well with large classes. For this reason I have, where appropriate, indicated the numbers in terms of groups, e.g. group(s) of about four, i.e. in a class of thirty this would mean six groups of five, or two groups of five and five groups of four. In a class of six this would be two groups of three or one of six.

5 **Target groups** Many of the activities can also be adapted to suit different target groups such as teachers, students or business people. I have indicated this at the end of the activity. The Index of activities on page viii highlights activities which are also useful for teacher training or for teaching business people.

6 **Follow-ons** Most activities include possible follow-on ideas, i.e. ways of using the materials the students have prepared. It is difficult to be precise about these as so much depends on what level we're working with, and the content of the materials that emerge. The follow-ons can happen in a later lesson.

7 **Checking and correcting** It is important to allow time for checking, correcting, and perhaps refining the students' materials for grammatical accuracy and appropriateness of language. In some cases we will want to make a thorough check, and in others a quick read through will be enough. I have indicated the checking stages in each activity. There are a number of different ways of doing it:

   a Students check and correct each others' work, using good dictionaries. They can consult us when they are not sure.

   b In some activities there is time for us to circulate and correct during class time, but this will depend on the numbers in the class.

c We can stop the activity at the correction stage, collect in their work and then continue the activity in another lesson.

SPIN-OFFS FOR THE TEACHER AND THE LEARNER

1 Learner generation of materials helps to create a positive and co-operative group spirit.

2 I have found that learners enjoy 'working on' their own material. It feels close and safe to them. Also it will not contain any words they don't know which might interfere with the controlled follow-on.

3 Teachers get a lot of feedback on what interests the learners, what kind of activities they like to learn by, and their linguistic problems or gaps.

4 Very few materials (usually none) are required.

5 It cuts down preparation time as the learners provide the materials. These two elements (4 and 5) are for me the criteria for a good recipe!

6 Most of the activities in this book can be done with a range of levels, and with multi-level classes. If students are creating and working on their own materials they naturally do this at their own level. When they are preparing activities for each other they can exchange with students of a similar level. In addition there are times when the higher level students can check and help correct the work of the lower level students, which frees us to check the work of the higher levels.

7 They provide excellent homework tasks which the students will feel more encouraged to do as their material will be used in class.

8 Using the learners' materials for other purposes helps to get over the problem that sometimes arises about the value of the free practice stage, i.e. 'We've just written a story, or had a discussion, but what good did it do me? I wasn't actually learning anything and I know I made a lot of mistakes.'

9 The teacher doesn't provide material which does not interest the learners.

10 Many such activities can be done with large groups and also on a one-to-one basis.

11 The time taken can be controlled depending on how or if you want to follow on the activity.

QUESTIONNAIRE

For you as a teacher, knower and facilitator

All the subsequent sections are tried and tested activities for you to use in the classroom. The rationale behind these activities will be much more apparent if you first spend time working through the questions on page 6. They form the basis of the rationale behind this book. In fact this book has come about as a direct result of using these questions with teachers on in-service training courses.

As teachers we have many options. Our decisions about these options are affected by many external and internal factors, such as class size, time of day, number of contact hours per week, age, and mood of students, our mood, level of students, students' learning strategies, course objectives and the objective of the lesson. It is all too easy for us to become set in our ways – to stop considering our options. I am not suggesting that any one option is the right one. Only that it is valuable and salutary for us to ask ourselves these questions, if only to remind ourselves that we do in fact have these options, and could and should consider them in our different teaching situations.

However, I am hoping that you will not regard the following activity as an option, but rather as an integral part of this book, serving as a bridge between the introduction and activities. Its purpose is to highlight major facets of teaching that we can open up to the student. There are a number of ways of answering these questions but I would suggest marking them from 1–5, according to either of the following systems:

Never me **1**   Sometimes me **2**   50/50 **3**   Usually me **4**
Always me **5**
Alternatively: Never my students **1**   Sometimes my students **2**
50/50 **3**   Usually my students **4**   Always my students **5**

1 Who chooses the topics?
2 Who chooses the activities?
3 Who prepares the activities/materials?
4 Who decides when to stop an activity?
5 Who do the students speak to?
6 Who do the students look at?
7 Who chooses the seating arrangements and moves the
   chairs and tables?
8 Who writes on the board?
9 Who cleans the board?
10 Who operates the equipment?
11 Who selects and explores structural gaps/problems?
12 Who selects the vocabulary?
13 Who spells out new words?
14 Who checks the work?
15 Who gives the instructions?
16 Who gives explanations?
17 Who writes/asks the comprehension questions?
18 Who answers questions asked by the students?
19 Who repeats what has been said if the others haven't heard it?
20 Who creates the silences?
21 Who breaks the silences?
22 Who gives dictations?
23 Who tells stories?
24 Who chooses the homework?
25 Who selects the pairs or groups?

© Longman Group UK Ltd 1990

SOME OF THE OPTIONS AND OPPORTUNITIES SUGGESTED BY THE QUESTIONNAIRE

1 Topics that teachers know nothing about can make the lesson much more interesting for them, and more demanding for the students.

2 Our students' 'personal luggage' must include some interesting and effective learning activities – some from home, some from classes in other subjects. This means we could sometimes give students the opportunity to suggest and set up their own activities.

3 A lot of the time we as teachers spend preparing materials can be fruitfully spent by the students doing the same thing, for example, preparing a grammar exercise.

4 Timing is one of the most difficult factors for me. Am I going too fast or too slowly for my students? I need their feedback on this.

5 I find particularly with new groups that they will only spontaneously interact if I am out of sight. Otherwise the tendency can be for them to use me as an interpreter or monitor.

6 I teach much better if I feel relaxed and comfortable. I don't always feel this if everybody is looking at me – as it were expectantly. This can make me panic and wonder 'what exactly are they expecting?'

7 This may seem unimportant but in my experience the success of a number of activities partially depends on the seating arrangements. In some cases it may be that the students have strong views about this. If we ignore these it could colour their attitude and approach to the activity. It also encourages the fallacy that the room belongs to the teacher rather than to all of us as a group. In some rooms it is impossible to move the tables and chairs. In others it is possible but teachers are understandably daunted by the chaos, time and noise involved. If the class accepts the advantages to them of exploiting different seating arrangements, they will be more likely to develop an efficient strategy for moving the furniture as and when necessary.

8 All I remember about my French teacher is her back view. With hindsight I realise that she was very unsure of herself and the blackboard was a safe retreat. See Comment 6. Brainstorming activities are just one opportunity for us to really let our students take over and help each other. If one or more of them are at the board, the teacher will naturally stop being the only evaluator and corrector.

9 This question may not be as trite as it appears. There are a number of ways of cleaning the board which can provide activities in learning, testing and expanding:

   a One student can wipe out one word of a sentence which is on the board for the class to replace with another word.

   b One student wipes out one letter of a word for the class to replace with another letter.

   c The class give the question that would elicit language on the board. When they give the right question the language is wiped off.

d The class put the new words on the board into sentences or make collocations. When they do this correctly the new words are wiped off.

10 My students are usually more proficient than I am in this area. When listening to cassettes it is sometimes less intimidating for our students if one of them is controlling the machine. They feel freer to ask their peers to rewind, stop, etc.

11 The content of a course can be selected by us all. If the students are given opportunities to make suggestions, it gives us as teachers feedback and it gives them more responsibility for their learning. When students are encouraged to explore language for themselves, they can often find patterns and explanations which help them, whereas if we do all the exploring, we put ourselves in the position of always having to explain what is found.

12 Vocabulary seems to be an area where we often fail our students. Historically, teachers have confined the teaching of vocabulary to providing it, and then leaving the students to learn it for themselves. Many of us have learnt vocabulary this way but I certainly remember it as being painful and requiring a lot of self-discipline. I think there should be times when the students provide the vocabulary and the teachers devote some classroom time to help them store, remember and activate It.

13 I like to make sure at an early stage that my students can handle the English alphabet effectively so that I am not the only one who ever spells out words or writes them on the board. It also helps me not to react like my own French teacher.

14 We learn by thinking, exploring and questioning. If teachers do all the checking, we may be 'stealing' a vital element of learning.

15 Giving instructions clearly is difficult, even in your mother tongue. Students need practice in this. Classroom instructions can be relayed. We can give the instructions for an activity to one student to then pass on to the class, or to pass on to another student who then relays them to another and so on.

16 We all have different ways of perceiving and understanding things. The kind of explanations we give may or may not help any of our students. The process of giving an explanation themselves helps our students to understand, consolidate and confirm their hypotheses, and encourages them to explore the patterns of the language.

17 Students seem to be much more interested in and therefore motivated by questions put to them by their peers. Perhaps this is the competitive element coming into play. Also the process of devising the questions is a valuable linguistic and comprehension activity.

18 There are many times when it does not have to be me who answers students' questions.

19 There are many times when it does not have to be me who reacts when someone says, 'Pardon?'.

20 It seems to me that classroom silences are created by the teacher – either advertently or inadvertently. One example of the latter is

when we ask a question which is either pointless, incomprehensible, too difficult or boring. Perhaps because we are aware of this, we are frightened of silences in our lessons. However, there can be pedagogical silence in the same way that there can be pedagogical sound. Learning and understanding need time for reflection, time to forget those around us and be in our own space.

21 When a student breaks a silence it is often with a question. This could be for confirmation of a point, or for other information. Whichever it is, this initiative on the part of the student can give us as teachers valuable information about how well they have understood, how they are feeling and whether or not they want more of the same thing.

22 There are three possibilities for who dictates:
   a teacher to students
   b students to teacher
   c students to students
   For many ideas on this read *Dictation* (Davis and Rinvolucri 1988).

23 The same three possibilities apply for who tells stories:
   a teacher to students
   b students to teacher
   c students to students
   For ideas read *Once Upon a Time* (Morgan and Rinvolucri 1983). Also look at the story telling and writing sections in this book.

24 Students will not choose anything they consider to be a waste of time or effort.

25 There are a number of possibilities:
   a teachers can choose the groups
   b students can choose the groups
   c split information activities
   d 'things in common' activities.

APPLICATIONS TO A COURSEBOOK

Some of the activities in this book can be applied to coursebook materials. I am not suggesting that this is always expedient but that it sometimes is. We need a battery of materials and techniques to draw on in our teaching and using student-generated activities is only one of them. Coursebooks can be an integral part of a course. Different ways of approaching and exploiting them can *personalise* them for us and our students. When this happens, students start to feel that the book is *theirs*, that they have an important contribution to make to the book, and that they *matter*. In fact the book becomes alive and so do the classroom, the students and the teacher.

For the sake of clarity I have taken a complete unit from a beginner's coursebook and have suggested ways of applying student-generated activities to it. However, I am not necessarily advocating that it is useful to use this approach throughout an entire unit. We can obviously pick and choose what is appropriate for our students and our teaching situation.

OPENING STRATEGIES

by Brian Abbs and Ingrid Freebairn (Longman 1982).

UNIT 8 PAGES 60–67

A Lead-in to the unit

What is a . . .? (Activity 4.3)

1 Ask the class to choose from the following alternatives: a hostess, an estate agent, a commuter, a waiter/waitress, a student, i.e. the 'people' they will come across in the unit.

2 Alternatively, give one of these 'people' to each group. They pass their statements to another group who tick the ten they like best and return this to the original group. They then rank them in order and put their list on the wall for everyone to see.

B Page 60 Dialogue: Part 1 (see below)

Miming/Dubbing (Activity 5.7)

1 Ask the students to cover the dialogue and focus only on the picture.

2 Put them into groups of four and ask them to position themselves like the picture. Give them time to think about the person they now are and the situation they are in. They can choose a name, lifestyle, etc.

3 Pair up groups. One group mime their conversation while the other group dub it. Then they can reverse.

▶◀ Dialogue: Part 1

DOUG: Hello! Come in! This is my wife, Liz. Liz, these are the people from Focus. Diana Trent and Paul Roberts.

LIZ: Hello. Nice to meet you. Was it far for you to come?

DIANA: No, I walked across the park. You're very near the park.

LIZ: Yes, we're lucky. I work in Kensington and I often cycle to work across the park.

PAUL: Oh, is it far?

LIZ: No, it only takes me about twenty-five minutes. I like the exercise. Doug's lazy. He always goes to work by underground.

DOUG: No, I don't. Not always.

LIZ: *(laughing)* No, you're right. You sometimes take a taxi! Come on, let's eat.

Are these true or false?
Doug and Liz live near the park.
Liz walks across the park to work.
Doug usually goes to work by underground.

Opening Strategies page 60

C Page 60 Set 1 Journeys (see below)

1 Ask the students to copy out the chart at the bottom but to fill in only the words that are in the left column.

2 They mill and ask each other the appropriate questions to complete the grid. Encourage them to try to find four different methods of transport. You may need to work on the question forms they are going to use before they do the activity.

3 This class-personalised grid can then be used for all the exercises on page 61 (see page 14).

1.		How do you get to work?
I	go by	bus. train. underground. car.
	drive. walk. cycle.	

How far is it?	
It's about	5 miles. (8 kilometres)
How long does it take?	
It takes about twenty minutes.	

Work with your partner. Look at the chart. One of you takes the part of the people in the chart, like this:

How do you get to work, Doug?
I usually go by underground.
How far is it?
It's about . . . .

Name:	Doug	Liz	Paul	Diana
Method of transport:	underground	cycle	car	walk
Distance to work:	3 miles (5 kilometres)	2 miles (3½ kilometres)	5 miles (8 kilometres)	1 mile (1½ kilometres)
Time:	20 minutes	25 minutes	10 minutes	15 minutes

Opening Strategies page 60

D Page 61 Exercise 4 (see page 14)
Student-generated Jazz Chants (Activity 4.1)

2. Talk and write about their journeys, like this:

Doug usually goes to work by underground. It's about 3 miles and it takes him about twenty minutes.

3. Ask your partner about his/her journey to work or school. Write about it in the same way.

4. Do you ever cycle to work, Liz?
Yes, often.

always   usually   often   sometimes   never

Name	cycle to work	late for work	take a taxi	work late in the evenings
Doug	never	sometimes	sometimes	always
Liz	often	never	never	often
Paul	sometimes	often	sometimes	never
Diana	never	sometimes	often	usually

In pairs, ask and answer questions, like this:

Do you ever cycle to work, Doug?
No, never.
Are you ever late for work?
Yes, sometimes.

Use both charts to write sentences about the people, like this:

Doug usually goes to work by underground, but he sometimes takes a taxi. He never cycles.
He's sometimes late for work. He always works late in the evenings.

Talk and write about yourself in the same way.

5.	How often do you go out?	Every			day. week.
		About	once twice three times	a	month. year.

Ask and answer in pairs:
How often do you
go to the cinema?   go swimming?   travel abroad?
theatre?   on holiday?   see your parents?
hairdresser's?   to church?   buy bread?

E Page 62 Dialogue: Part 2 (see below)
(Activity 8.4**a**)

1 Ask each student to pick one keyword from each exchange and write them in a list on a clean piece of paper. It's important to set a short time limit for this so that they have to skim (about two minutes).

2 They exchange lists and write their own dialogues.

⊙⊙ Dialogue: Part 2 [＿＿＿＿＿]

DIANA: It all looks delicious!
DOUG: Would you like chicken or beef, or both?
DIANA: I'd like beef, please.
DOUG: And would you like salad with it?
DIANA: Yes, please.
DOUG: What sort would you like?
DIANA: I don't know. What is there?
DOUG: There's potato salad, bean salad, green salad.
DIANA: I'd like some of each, please. Thanks.
DOUG: OK, Diana. Let's talk about your film. What's it about?

Answer:
What meat is there?
What salad is there?
What does Diana have?

Opening Strategies page 62

F Page 62 Menu (see below)

Vocabulary Sheets (Activity 7.2)

1 Don't let them see the printed menu.
2 Write the four categories on the board.
3 Divide the class into four groups and give each group one of the categories.

Opening Strategies page 62

G Page 64 Set 3 House and Home (see below)

Personalise

1 Let the students see the diagram and then ask them to do a similar diagram for their own home. This will be the basis for the activities on page 65 (see page 18).

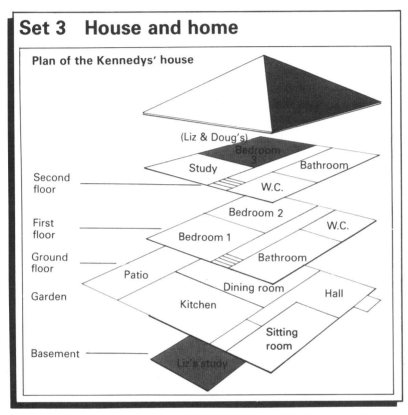

Set 3   House and home

Plan of the Kennedys' house

(Liz & Doug's)
Bedroom 3

Study   Bathroom

Second floor   W.C.

Bedroom 2

First floor   W.C.

Bedroom 1

Ground floor   Bathroom

Patio

Garden   Dining room   Hall

Kitchen

Sitting room

Basement   Liz's study

Opening Strategies page 64

H Page 65 Question practice (see page 18)

Ask Me My Questions (Activity 5.3)

1 Tell the group they are potential buyers of a house.

2 Ask them to write 10–15 questions they would want to ask the agent/ owner before they saw the house.

3 Divide the group into pairs or small groups. They give each other their questions to check.

4 Student A becomes the owner/agent. Student B (or small group) asks Student A the questions s/he has written. They can supplement them with other questions if they wish.

5 Repeat with Student B, etc.

1. How many floors are there?
There are three altogether, and a basement.

Look at the plan of the Kennedys' house. Ask and answer in pairs, like this:
How many bedrooms are there?
     studies
     bathrooms
     toilets (W.C.)
     rooms (apart from the hall, the bathrooms and toilets)

2.	Where's the kitchen? It's on the ground floor.	Where are the toilets? There's one on the first floor and another on the second floor.

Look at the plan again and ask and answer about these rooms:
the kitchen   the dining room   Liz's study
the sitting room   Liz and Doug's   the other bedrooms
the bathrooms   bedroom

3. What colour is the study in the basement? It's brown.

Find the colours:
     black
     blue
     green
     orange
     red
     white
     yellow

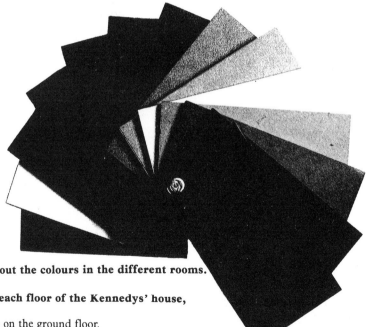

Ask and answer questions about the colours in the different rooms.

4. Tell your partner about each floor of the Kennedys' house, like this:
     There's a big kitchen on the ground floor.

Talk and then write about the other floors of the house, like this:
     There's/There are . . .

Writing
Write two or three sentences about your home.

I Page 66 Writing (see below) Mutual Dictation Stories (Activity 3.2)

J Page 66 Listening (see below) Duplicate Listening (Activity 2.1)

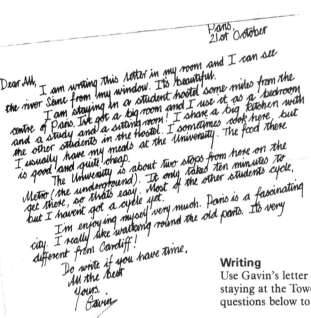

Paris,
21st October

Dear Ali,
I am writing this letter in my room and I can see the river Seine from my window. It's beautiful.
I am staying in a student hostel some miles from the centre of Paris. I've got a big room and I use it as a bedroom and a study and a sitting room! I share a big kitchen with the other students in the hostel. I sometimes cook here, but I usually have my meals at the University. The food there is good and quite cheap.
The University is about two stops from here on the Metro (the underground). It only takes ten minutes to get there, so that's easy. Most of the other students cycle, but I haven't got a cycle yet.
I'm enjoying myself very much. Paris is a fascinating city. I really like walking round the old parts. It's very different from Cardiff!
Do write if you have time.
All the best
Yours,
Gavin

Which is the right answer?

1. Gavin is studying in a) Cardiff at the moment.
   b) Paris.
2. He is living a) in the centre of Paris.
   b) in the country.
   c) near the centre of Paris.
3. He has a) one room.
   b) two rooms.
   c) three rooms.
4. He a) sometimes eats at the hostel.
   b) never
   c) always
5. He usually a) walks to the University every morning.
   b) goes by underground.
   c) cycles.
6. He likes a) walking round the old parts of Paris.
   b) walking in the country.
   c) Cardiff.

Writing

Use Gavin's letter to help you to write a letter to a friend. Imagine you are staying at the Tower Hotel in London for a week's holiday. Use the questions below to help you plan your letter.

PARAGRAPH 1:	Where are you writing the letter?
	Where are you staying?
PARAGRAPH 2:	What can you see from your window?
	What is the hotel like?
	What is your hotel room like?
PARAGRAPH 3:	How far is the hotel from the West End?
	How do you get to the West End?
	How long does it take you?
PARAGRAPH 4:	Do you like London?
	What do you like doing most?
END THE LETTER LIKE THIS:	
	Please write if you have time.
	All the best.
	Yours,
	(Your first name)

Listening

Lynette lives in Brighton. One place she likes to visit is the Brighton Pavilion. This beautiful building was once the summer house of the Prince Regent in the late eighteenth and early nineteenth century. Listen to Lynette and note down the rooms she talks about.

K Page 67 Exercises 3 and 4 (see below)

Find Someone Who (Activity 1.3)

1 Ask the students to write on the top of a piece of paper: *Find Someone Who . . .?*

2 Underneath this they write the statements which they have to transform from the questions in the two exercises, e.g. 1 *is late for work.*

3 They mill and reformulate the questions to try and find a name for each statement.

L Page 67 Grammar (see below)

Word Order (Activity 6.3)

They could first of all use the examples given and then make up their own.

---

3. Answer about your routine (Open exercise)

Are you ever late for work?

(Yes, sometimes.)

Do you ever take a taxi?

(No, never.)

1. Are you ever late for work or school?
2. Do you ever take a taxi?
3. Do you ever walk to work or school?
4. Do you ever work at weekends?
5. Do you ever go home for lunch?
6. Do you ever travel in your job?

4. Answer about your life (Open exercise)

How often do you get up before seven?

(About once a week.)

1. How often do you get up before seven?
2. How often do you go to bed after midnight?
3. How often do you watch TV?
4. How often do you go to a concert?
5. How often do you buy a new record?

Grammar

What (sort of)	salad vegetables	would you like?

I'd like	some green salad, some peas,	please.

How far is it	to	work? London?
It's about		a mile. half a mile. thirty miles.

How often	do	you they	go abroad? cycle to work?
	does	he she	

How	do	you	get to work?
	does	he she	

How long does the journey take	(you)? (him/her)?
It takes about	ten minutes. half an hour. quarter of an hour. an hour.

I	usually	go	bus.
He She	often sometimes always never	goes by	underground. train.

Every		day.
Once Twice Three times	a	week. month. year.

How many bathrooms are there?				
There's	one another	on the	ground first second	floor.
There are two				

What colour	is	the bathroom? the bedroom?	It's	blue. red.

Opening Strategies page 67

CLASSROOM ACTIVITIES

Before using these activities it is important to read the information on page 3.

They are classified under different chapter headings but there is inevitably an overlap as some activities would fit under more than one heading. For example, many of the activities use all four skills. Where useful I have suggested follow-on activities, but these always depend on the moment, i.e. the level, time, teaching objective and the material that the students have generated.

Above all, these activities should be treated as sparking plugs. They are there for teachers and students to exploit, adapt, enjoy, learn from, teach from, in any way that is appropriate for the class at the time.

CHAPTER 1

Ice-breakers

These activities help a group to learn each others' names and get to know something about each other, and help us as teachers to get a flavour of our group in terms of their abilities and interests. They take longer than some other ice-breakers as the students need time to prepare them. However, this time is spent productively, so as a by-product to the activities being ice-breakers, the students are practising and using a variety of language skills.

1.1

LEVEL
Elementary +

TIME
30–45 minutes

MATERIALS
Board or paper for each group

NUMBERS
At least 2 groups, maximum of 8 in each group

CROSSWORD NAMES

Procedure

1 One person in each group writes their name in big letters across the board. It's best to start with a name of about eight letters. The other members of the group then add their names in the format of a crossword puzzle. The finished crossword could look like the one in Fig. 1.

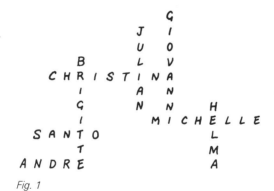

Fig. 1

Fig. 2

2 Each group writes out a blank copy of the format of their crossword, i.e. without the names, but with the squares indicated and the appropriate squares numbered (see Fig. 2).

3 They write numbered clues for each name in their crossword to give another group. These could be a play on the words or just a simple description of the person – depending on the level of your class, for example:

a 3 across   The tallest person here.

b 3 down   Mozart wrote about him.

c 4 down   H followed by a mixed meal.

4 You check their clues to make sure you can understand them.

5 Each group tries to solve the crossword of another group.

ACKNOWLEDGEMENT

Stage 1 of this activity has been around a few years, but I was introduced to it by Seth Lindstromberg.

SELF-DIRECTED INTERVIEWS

Procedure

1 Each person writes down 3–5 topics that they would like their partner to ask them about. These can be as personal or impersonal as they wish, but the objective is to help their partner find out information about them.

2 Partners exchange their lists of topics and interview each other, using the topic list as a basis for their interview. The interviewer takes some notes so that they will be able to relay the information to another student later. Set a time limit for this phase, about three minutes per topic.

3 Pairs then go into groups of four and tell the other pair about each other.

4 All the information is collated by the class. They elect a secretary and tell this secretary what categories to write as headings on the board. They then call out to the secretary the details to put under the different headings. If you prefer you can do this phase in smaller groups using a piece of paper. The board might look something like Fig. 3.

1.2

LEVEL
Lower intermediate +

TIME
45 minutes

MATERIALS
None

NUMBERS
Minimum 2, no maximum

JOBS	AMBITIONS	TRAVELS	SKILLS	IMPORTANT POSSESSIONS
Receptionist	Be rich	Greece	Tennis	a ring
Engineer	Pass my exams	USA	Piano	a camera
Teacher	Go to Peru	Hungary	Telling jokes	a piano
Secretary	Be a pilot	Egypt	Cooking	a dog

Fig. 3

FOLLOW-ONS

a practising structures, e.g.:

can/can't	Y can play the piano
has/doesn't have	X has a camera
has been	X has been to Greece
likes/doesn't like	X doesn't like travelling
is good at	Y is good at water-skiing
adverbs of frequency	Y often plays the sax

b writing summaries, e.g.:
A summary of the different countries the group has visited.

c vocabulary building, e.g.:
Adjectives to describe the important possessions.

d job descriptions

e personality profiles

The uses for this material will obviously depend on what emerges from the interviews, and the level of the students. My list is far from exhaustive.

NOTES

a This activity can stop at any point after Stage 2.

b Interviewing is an important language teaching activity – particularly for students who will be taking English oral exams. It is usually the interviewer who controls the content matter. This technique is useful for preparing students for this, and allows them to make more of a contribution.

VARIATION

Teacher training application   Ask each person to write five aspects of teaching they would like to be asked about.

ACKNOWLEDGEMENT
I first came across Stages 1 and 2 of this activity in *Keep Talking* (Klippel 1985).

I HOPE I FIND SOMEONE WHO . . .

This is a variation on the well-known 'Find Someone Who . . .', the difference being that the students do all the preparation and select the topics. The usual procedure is for the teacher to prepare a list of about ten statements. The students must then transform these statements into questions to ask each other, while milling round the room. The statements often focus on a particular tense or subject area. The activity stops when someone has found a name to match each statement. For example, to practise the past tense:

Find someone who . . .   and write their name here:
a smoked at school.   _____
b bought a car last year.   _____
c spent last summer abroad.   _____
d lost something last month.   _____

Procedure

1 For this activity the stem is *I hope I find someone who. . . .* It is best to start with some examples of your own, such as:

In this group I hope I find someone who:
a likes the theatre.
b has a boat.
c speaks Polish.

2 Ask your students to write their own hopes about the group. I usually suggest they write 8–10. After each one they leave a space for a name as in the example above.

3 Allow time for checking their statements for accuracy. This could be done in pairs with you helping when needed.

4 Let them circulate and fill in names for as many of their items as possible. You may want to insist that they ask the questions rather than just show each other their sentences.

5 They talk to the people whose names they have on their papers and ask detailed questions about the items they have responded to.

NOTES

a This activity can also be used as a guided practice for any language point you want your students to practise. For example, students could be asked to write ten statements all in the past tense, as in the example.

b Application to a coursebook See Section 2, K.

1.3

LEVEL
Lower
intermediate +

TIME
30 minutes

MATERIALS
None

NUMBERS
Minimum 4, no
maximum

1.4

LEVEL
Elementary +

TIME
This depends entirely on the number in a group. For 10 people allow 15 minutes

MATERIALS
None

NUMBERS
Group(s) of 5–10

WHAT I LIKE ABOUT YOU IS . . .
Procedure

1 Get everybody to sit in a circle. If there is only one group join in the circle yourself.
2 Starting with the person on your left, Student A, say something that you like about the person, such as, *What I like about you is the colour of your hair and your laugh.*
3 This continues in an anti-clockwise direction with each person in turn saying something that they like about Student A. When everyone has said something then Student A says something s/he likes about her/himself.
4 Student A starts the next round by saying something they like about the student on their left and so on round the circle as before.
5 This continues until everyone has been talked about by everyone – including you if you are in the circle.

NOTE
A very positive start for a group.

ACKNOWLEDGEMENT
I experienced this activity on a drama workshop run by Denis Noonan.

1.5

LEVEL
Elementary +

TIME
20 minutes

MATERIALS
A4 paper and Sellotape or pins

NUMBERS
Minimum 2, no maximum

INTEREST PIES
Procedure

1 Ask the students to use a clean piece of paper, about A4 size, and to draw a big circle which they will then make into a pie chart.
2 They fill in their pie charts with anything that is important to them and about them, using a bigger slice for the areas which are more important to them.
3 Pin or stick the charts on to their fronts and then everyone mills round looking at each others' charts and asking questions about anything they would like to know more about. Fig. 4 shows how this exercise can work.

NOTES

a This simple activity generates a lot of natural social chitchat and interest, which is made easier because the subject matter is provided.
b It helps a new group to find like-minded people and new ideas.
c I always like opportunities to get away from vertical lists.

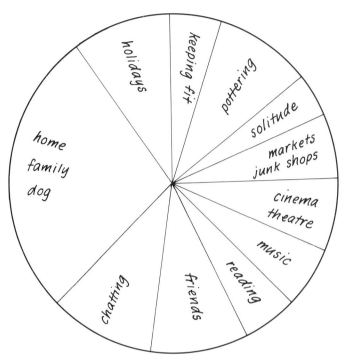

Fig. 4

VARIATIONS

1 The pie chart could be used for revision or a recap of the previous lesson(s). Students could be asked to fill in the activities they liked most or found most useful. This would also serve as feedback for the teacher.

2 Teacher training application   The pie chart could be filled in with aspects of teaching which people enjoy or are good at – or conversely don't enjoy or have problems with.

ACKNOWLEDGEMENT
Wojtek Krajewski

CHAPTER 2

Comprehension activities

Listening and reading comprehension activities tend to be teacher-centred and also to smack of exams. Learners seem to care more about answering questions asked by their peers. They like to catch each other out and they don't want to be caught out. In the process of devising questions themselves they gain valuable extra language practice. In fact, it can be fun.

2.1

LEVEL
Elementary +

TIME
45–60 minutes

MATERIALS
Listening material suitable for your class. Length 5–7 minutes, e.g the news, a short story, a dialogue, a song. Cassette player(s)

NUMBERS
Minimum 4. An even number of groups of about 6 people per group

DUPLICATE LISTENING

This activity is based on listening (or reading – see Variation 1) material, but involves listening and speaking and writing. The listening (or reading) phase is entirely controlled by the students.

Procedure

1 Divide the class into an even number of groups of about six people per group, e.g. in a class of 30 divide the students into two groups of eight and two of seven.

2 Each group listens to their recording. If you don't have enough space or equipment for them to do this at the same time, stagger the listening sessions so that one group listens while the other group(s) work on something else such as reading material (see Variation 1). Leave the groups to listen at their own pace, pausing and rewinding whenever necessary. Tell them they must all take notes and help each other by sharing and discussing what they have understood. Make it clear that there is a time limit to discourage them from trying to write a transcript or complete sentences, rather than simple notes of topics, names, numbers and times. When they have finished, or your time limit is up, remove the tape.

3 Each group prepares a set of 10–15 questions to ask one of the other groups. Every student in the group must make a copy and must know the answers to their questions, and the questions must be correctly formed. If they have other questions they don't know the answers to, they can add them as extras.

4 Check their questions for grammatical accuracy and to make sure they can actually be answered from the text.

5 Form the students into pairs from different groups. All the pairs start at the same time and ask each other their questions. It is important that within the pairs A and B should ask their questions alternately, as some questions may be duplicated. In this way they each have an equal chance to get duplicated questions in first. If they can't agree

about an answer, they should write the question on the board.

6 The class listen to the tape together to find the answers to any questions on the board. At this stage you might even want to add some yourself.

FOLLOW-ONS

a Each original group or pair acts out a role play or interview based on some or all of the material. A variation would be for them to include one piece of false information in the role play for the other group to detect.

b They rewrite one news topic.

c Each group writes the questions they have just answered. This depends on them having made notes of their answers. They then compare them to the original questions.

NOTE

Application to a coursebook   See Section 2, J.

VARIATIONS

1 This technique is also useful for a longer reading text. The groups have the same text (perhaps in their coursebook, or a text written on the blackboard). They read it together in their groups, sharing their understanding of it and taking short notes, i.e. words, not sentences. You can limit these to only names and numbers. When the time limit is up you take the text away (or rub it out), and they then prepare the questions in the same way as in the listening activity.

2 **Teacher training application**   The task in Stage 3 can be to devise other activities to go with the text, such as a grid to be filled in, a matching activity or a jigsaw activity.

ACKNOWLEDGEMENT
First published in *Practical English Teaching* (Deller 1986).

STUDENT PRE-TEXT QUESTIONS
Procedure

1 Give the class the title or theme of the text, but don't let them see or hear the text at this point.

2 Ask the class to write individually five questions they hope will be answered in the text. For example, for the title 'Airport Stolen' some possible questions are:
  a Who stole it?
  b How was it stolen?
  c Why was it stolen?
  d Were they caught?
  e How many people were there?

2.2

LEVEL
Lower intermediate +

TIME
45 minutes

MATERIALS
A reading or listening text

NUMBERS
Minimum 2

3 At this point it is interesting to compare the questions. This can be done as a group with a secretary writing them up on the board, or by mingling, or just in pairs. At the same time the questions can be checked by you and the group for mistakes.

4 If Stage 3 has been done as a group activity the group now guesses the answers.

5 Hand out or play the text and let the students try to answer their questions.

FOLLOW-ON

Any questions that can't be answered are used as a source for writing another text, or for rewriting the original. If in the above example questions (c) and (e) are not answered by the text, students could add this information to it, changing the text where necessary.

NOTE

The process of searching for the answers to their own questions is a natural and enjoyable way of practising the skill of scanning.

2.3

LEVEL
Lower
intermediate +

TIME
45 minutes

MATERIALS
A selection of
newspapers in the
target language (not
necessarily current)
– one paper per
person/pair/group

NUMBERS
Minimum 2, no
maximum

NEWSPAPER SEARCH

Procedure

1 If there are four or more people in the class put them into pairs or small groups.

2 Let each group choose a newspaper.

3 Ask each group to skim through their newspaper and write about eight questions for another group to answer. I limit them to not more than two questions per article so as to encourage them to look at more of the newspaper. It is important to set a time limit at this stage so that the questions don't become too difficult – about twenty minutes for eight questions with an intermediate level class.

4 You check their questions for accuracy and to make sure they are not too difficult to answer.

5 The groups leave their questions on top of their newspaper.

6 The groups rotate one place in a clockwise direction and then scan through the other group's newspaper to write the answers to that group's questions.

7 The groups return to their original questions and check the other group's written answers. They discuss any answers they disagree with, with the group who wrote them.

FOLLOW-ON

They cut up and mix their questions with the relevant answers and give them to another group for a matching activity.

NOTE

This activity reflects how most people actually read a newspaper. It's not the norm just to focus on one article as we often do in our classes.

STUDENTS AS EDITORS

Procedure

1 Students work individually, pairs or in small groups.
2 Tell them they are the editors of the newspaper that they choose from your selection.
3 They select an article, advertisement, letter or group of headlines from the paper and write editing instructions for another group who will be the reporters or journalists. The instructions can include additions, deletions, changes of style or layout, lexical changes, who should be interviewed, and how it should be followed up. You may want to limit the number of instructions they give. Here are some instructions as examples:
   - Give more details of his background.
   - Cut out the bit about his mother.
   - Headline too long.
   - Make the style less familiar – more formal.
   - Don't use the word 'spy'.
   - Try to interview his wife.
   - Put the bit about his money nearer the beginning.
4 You check their instructions.
5 Groups exchange instructions and carry out the instructions they receive.
6 They submit their work to their editor for approval. At this point the editors may want to ask you for your opinion or help.

FOLLOW-ONS

a Put the articles on the wall and deal out the instructions. The students have to match the instructions to the article.
b The editors' instructions and corresponding edited versions are displayed for everyone to read.

VARIATIONS

1 This exercise can also be used with video. For many ideas on this see *Video* (Cooper, Maley and Rinvolucri, 1989).
2 **Business application**   Use the business sections of the newspapers (as in Activity 3.1).

ACKNOWLEDGEMENT
The idea of editing published material has been around for a long time. but I was introduced to this activity by Teresa Doguelli in Poland.

2.4

LEVEL
Intermediate +

TIME
45 minutes

MATERIALS
A selection of newspapers in the target language (not necessarily current)

NUMBERS
Minimum 2, no maximum

CHAPTER 3

Story telling

We often ask our students to tell stories. Sometimes there are problems because it is hard for anyone to feel inspired and creative at the drop of a hat, particularly when this has to be in a foreign language. The three activities in this section give the students a lot of support.

3.1

LEVEL
Lower
intermediate +

TIME
20 minutes

MATERIALS
None

NUMBERS
Minimum 2, no
maximum

MY KINGDOM

Procedure

I use this title as the activity is based on a party game of the same name.
1 Divide the class into two groups and send group A out of the room.
2 Tell group A that group B are going to make up a story. Group A's task will be to ask yes/no questions to discover the story. Stress that they should try to find out as many details as possible, such as descriptions of the people and places involved. Give them time to prepare some questions.
3 Tell group B what you have told group A. But then tell them that they don't have to make up a story. All they have to do is to think up a code to determine whether to answer *yes* or *no*. I try not to influence this except to ensure that the code won't produce too many *no* answers. Here are some examples of codes my groups have used:
    a *No* to every third question.
    b *No* if the question ends in a vowel.
    c *Yes* if the question includes a word with a double letter, e.g. *accident.*
    d *Yes* if there are less than seven words in the question.
    I had the proviso that the answers must be logically consistent so they must temporarily break their code if a *yes* or *no* answer would contradict a previous answer.
4 Students in group A pair off with students in group B. Group A students ask their question and group B students respond according to their code. In this way each pair creates an entirely different story, which emerges from the *yes* answers.
5 Group B should make a note of the story as it evolves. It is important that at this stage group A still believe that group B have prepared a story.
6 Group B let group A into their secret.
7 Pairs retell their stories. This can be done in a number of ways.
    a Pairs tell their stories to the whole class.
    b Pairs mill around telling other pairs their stories.
    c Pairs write up their stories and display them, or pass them round.

The following story emerged in one of my classes. This is the original oral version which I took down verbatim:

Once upon a time two women and a dog walking one winter morning on an icy lake covered with snow. Lovely morning and landscape. They couldn't see the hole in the lake because of the snow. One of them fell down the hole into the water. The other told her to hold up the ice while she went for help as soon as possible. The other cried. The dog stayed with the lady in the ice. She got the firepolice very quickly because they had warm clothes and food. The lady was rescued. She was rich and gave a present to these firepolice in this village.

FOLLOW-ONS

This student-generated material can be used as source material to practise many language points. These can't be predicted with any certainty as different materials will be suitable for different kinds of exploitation. Possibilities include: conditionals, linkers, interrupting, asking for detailed information, changing the time, summarising or expanding. The story in this example was useful for practising third conditionals and for building vocabulary by adding adjectives and descriptions. In addition we built up the sentences and added linkers.

NOTES

a Group A can be given time as a group to decipher the code.
b If you prefer, Stage 4 can be done as a whole-class activity. Group A take it in turns to ask a question to group B students who take it in turns to answer. In this case only one story will emerge.
c I've only ever used the activity once per group.
d There is a danger that very personal stories may emerge. This happened in one of my classes and the student concerned was very upset when he thought the other group had made up a story about him. Since then I have always started by telling group A that the story of group B is not about them.

VARIATIONS

1 The instructions to group A can vary. Rather than tell them that group B is preparing a story, you can tell them that group B has invented a mythical country, a job, a family or a particular character. Group A must ask questions to find out as much about this as possible.
2 **Business application** Tell group A that group B have designed a new product, or a new company, or a new job, or a new marketing strategy. Group A must find out as much about it as possible.

3.2

LEVEL
Elementary +

TIME
30 minutes

MATERIALS
Pieces of A4 paper

NUMBERS
Minimum 2, no maximum

MUTUAL DICTATION STORIES

Procedure

1 In pairs A and B sit opposite each other as far away from other pairs as possible to avoid disturbance.

2 Each student writes *A* and *B* on alternate lines on a piece of A4 paper, as shown in Fig. 5.

3 Tell the class that As must only write in the A spaces and Bs in the B spaces, so that they each end up with only half the story. It's important to emphasise this as I find they are tempted to write everything.

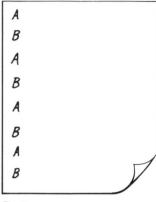

Fig. 5

4 As a class they decide on the opening sentence of a story. The more open this is the better, for example, 'There was once a man who lived in a wood', is less wide open than 'She left quickly', or 'They couldn't understand'.

5 Only As write the first line. Then privately, in pairs, A thinks up and dictates a second sentence to B. Only Bs write this. Then B dictates a third sentence, and so on, so that finally each student has written every other sentence of the story which was given to them by their partner.

6 They check each other's scripts for any mistakes and to make sure that their partner wrote what they dictated. They can ask you about any points of grammar or vocabulary they might want to improve.

7 Pairs practise reading their stories, as dramatically as they like. They can choose to read either the lines they wrote or the lines they dictated.

8 Pairs share stories. How this is done will depend on the size of the class. One way is for pairs to mingle and exchange. It seems to work better if they stand for this phase.

FOLLOW-ONS

a Pairs give another pair only student A's sentences and the other pair fills in the missing alternate sentences.

b Two pairs combine all or part of their stories.

c Add three words to each sentence in their stories.

d Rewrite as a dialogue.

e Pairs cut up their sentences and give to another pair to reorder.

f Pairs give each other their stories with the beginning, middle or end omitted. The other pair complete the missing section.

g Pairs delete every seventh word of their story for another pair to fill in.

h They add suitable linkers.

i Distribute the B sheets round the class (one between two). One pair reads the first B line. The rest of the class then ask questions to find out the rest of the story. Depending on numbers, this could be done as a whole-class activity or in small groups.

NOTES

a This is one of my favourite activities. It isn't threatening because of the shared responsibility and stimulation, and students find it rewarding and challenging.

b In the original form of this activity the teacher provides the material which the students dictate to each other, i.e. student A is given lines 1, 3, 5, and student B is given lines 2, 4, 6. This is a very effective controlled practice activity. However, there are many teaching situations where the class size is too large to produce the material without access to a photocopier. A corrected student-generated mutual dictation could be given to other groups as the material for a standard mutual dictation. The teacher must spend time correcting them, but saves a lot of time by not having to produce them.

c Application to a coursebook   See Section 2, I.

VARIATIONS

1 Instead of a story, students could write a dialogue (which could then be turned into indirect speech), a poem, words for a song, a recipe, a letter, a set of instructions, or information on a particular topic. This is good for ESP.

2 Teacher training application   Ask the group to dictate sentences to each other about a particular teaching technique, such as the use of dictations, or the pros and cons of this activity. They could also think of follow-on activities for this kind of mutual dictation.

ACKNOWLEDGEMENT
This activity is an extension of a mutual dictation which originated from the Bell School, Bath. The teacher training application came as a direct influence from *Loop Input* (Woodward 1988).

3.3

LEVEL
Lower
intermediate +

TIME
60 minutes

MATERIALS
One piece of paper,
about A4 size, per
student

NUMBERS
At least 2 groups of
about 6 per group

GROUP CHAIN STORIES

Procedure

1 Put groups round a table, each student with a piece of A4 paper and a pen.

2 Each group decides on the first line of a story. Encourage them to make this as open as possible, as in Stage 2 of the previous activity.

3 Everybody in the group writes this first line at the top of their piece of paper. Then individually they add the next sentence. The papers are then passed round to the person on the left. Each person then writes the sentence to follow the previous one on their new paper. This continues until the pages get back to where they began so that the first and last sentences of the stories are written by the same person.

4 Everybody checks their story for mistakes or improvements. If they want to change or correct anything they must consult the student who wrote it before doing so. If necessary they can ask you to arbitrate or advise. Check as many as possible yourself.

5 In their groups they each read out their final versions and vote on the one they want to present to the other group(s). I always check at least this one myself.

6 They rehearse their presentations. I use the word 'present' the story to the rest of the class in my instructions as it is open to a wide interpretation. Different groups will choose different formats, e.g. each person reads the line they wrote; one person narrates while the others mime; the group act out the story (with or without a narrator). I always suggest that as many of them should be involved as possible. In practice, I have usually found that they all take part, but that is their choice.

FOLLOW-ONS

The same as for Mutual Dictation Stories, Activity 3.2.

NOTES

a Some of the best role plays I have seen have resulted from this activity. Even the more inhibited students seem happy and relaxed performing materials that they have been partially, but not wholly, responsible for. On one notable occasion the sketches that evolved were later performed in an end-of-course revue, totally unprompted by me.

b Another bonus of a group chain story is that in Stage 5 everybody listens to every story enthusiastically. We all have an egocentric streak which motivates us to listen to find out what happened to our contributions.

VARIATIONS

1 The technique could be used to generate dialogues.

2 **Business or ESP application** Students could focus on their parti-

cular area of interest, e.g. the opening line could be 'There are a number of stages involved in launching a new product'.

3 **Teacher training application**   Teachers could focus on a particular teaching point, e.g. they could choose to write about different ways of using stories in the classroom.

ACKNOWLEDGEMENTS
I first saw Stages 1–3 of this activity done by Roger Woodham on a training workshop in Poland.

CHAPTER 4

Creative drills

These activities aim to get over the perennial problem of learners needing the opportunity for repetition, but feeling bored or patronised in the process.

4.1

LEVEL
Beginner +

TIME
15 minutes

MATERIALS
None

NUMBERS
Group(s) of about 10

STUDENT-GENERATED JAZZ CHANTS
Procedure

This can be used to practise any language point. The teacher provides a framework, for example, to practice the present perfect:

1 Write on the board:

A: Have you ever . . .?
B: No, never.

2 Tell the students to complete A's question. They will be asking it to their neighbour, B, who must answer *No, never*. It's important that they realise this so that they think up questions which are bound to elicit the answer *No*. It's a good idea to give an example to illustrate this and for them to hear a rhythm, e.g. *Have you ever slept in a fridge?*

3 While they are doing this, you write the framework for the jazz chant on the board. For example:

A: Have you ever . . .?
B: No, never, no, never.
Class: S/He's never . . . in her/his life.

There are three criteria for the framework:
a Everyone should join in saying at least one line of it.
b It should be easy to say rhythmically.
c It allows for transformations if appropriate. (In this example, from second to third person).

4 Student A asks their question to student B on their left who responds with the given answer. Then the whole class say line 3. Student B then continues with their question to the person on their left, and so on round the circle.

NOTES
a When they get used to the technique, students can design the framework themselves.
b **Application to a coursebook**   See Section 2, D.

ACKNOWLEDGEMENT

The idea of jazz chants comes from *Jazz Chants* (Graham 1978).

SPLIT STRUCTURES
Procedure

This can be used to repeat and practise any structures which have two parts, such as conditionals or tags. For example, to practise *was going to* + excuse:

1 Divide the group(s) into A and B. Ask everyone in group A to write the first part of a sentence with *I was going to*, e.g. *I was going to give up teaching.*
2 Everyone in group B writes one excuse beginning with *but . . .*, e.g. *but I couldn't be bothered.* Stages 1 and 2 are done individually and privately.
3 Ask one member of group A to read their sentence out. If someone in group B has an appropriate follow-on they read it out. The first person keeps repeating their sentence until everyone in group B who has an appropriate response has had a chance to say it. Then a second person in group A reads their sentence and the process is repeated. If, when all group A's sentences have been read out, there is a member of group B who has not been able to read their 'but' clause, they read it now and the first group thinks of an appropriate beginning.

NOTE

This activity can produce some bizarre and amusing combinations which help the structure to stick, e.g. *I was going to cook the lunch . . . but I lost my spade.* This isn't usually the case with the materials we *give* our students.

4.2

LEVEL
Elementary +

TIME
15 minutes

MATERIALS
None

NUMBERS
Group(s) of about 12

4.3

LEVEL
Lower
intermediate +

TIME
30 minutes

MATERIALS
None

NUMBERS
Minimum 2, no
maximum

WHAT IS A . . .?

Procedure

1 Write 'What is a . . .?' on the board. Tell the class that the ending of the question is a person, e.g. a teacher, tourist, politician, Spaniard, husband. In other words it doesn't necessarily have to be a job. The class decide on the ending.

2 The following stages can be done individually, in pairs or in small groups, depending on numbers. Write on the board, for example:

A tourist is a person who:
1 _____
2 _____
3 _____ etc.

Each group writes twenty statements with this format. I stipulate as many as twenty so as to get an interesting variety.

3 You check their lists for grammatical accuracy.

4 Each group passes their list to another group for them to select the ones they like best. I set a limit here, depending on how many groups I have, but the class total of selected statements should be in the region of ten.

5 The groups tell each other which statements they have selected by dictating them. While one group is dictating, the other groups write down the statements, each on a separate slip of paper. (One set of statements per group is enough.) Here is an unedited example of the selection of statements the groups in an intermediate class made from the heading 'What is a tourist?'

A tourist is a person who:
- is in many cases drunken.
- disturbs the natives.
- feels like a 'King or Queen'.
- is very intolerant to the native traditions.
- has often adventures with the foreign police.
- can loose his heart in Heidelberg.
- (American) takes three days for Europe.
- needs a valid passport.
- buys luggage before starting.
- takes always photographs.

6 Each group ranks these statements in order of the ones they like best, and everybody in the group makes a copy of their group's decision.

7 Jigsaw activity. Re-form groups so that there is one person from each original group in the new groups. They try to reach an agreed order.

FOLLOW-ONS

a Each group could choose one item to act out, e.g. 'is very intolerant to the native traditions'.

b Each group could write a dialogue for one of the items, e.g. 'buys luggage before starting'.

c They could put the statements into reported speech, e.g. *Group A said that a tourist . . .*

NOTES

a The jigsaw stage could be omitted.

b I suggest using slips of paper in Stage 4 as that makes the ranking process easier and more fun.

c This is an excellent activity to reinforce third person *'s'*, the use of *who* for people, and adverbs of frequency.

d **Application to a coursebook**   See Section 2, A.

VARIATIONS

1 With low levels you can brainstorm vocabulary between Stages 1 and 2.

2 **Teacher training application**   Teachers could use headings such as: 'What is a . . . teacher/learner/coursebook/, group, good lesson, classroom, difficult student, blackboard, good learner' etc.

3 **Business application**   Use the activity to focus only on relevant jobs, e.g. manager.

CHAPTER 5

Fluency activities

These activities allow and encourage the students to improvise and use the target language spontaneously.

LEVEL
Intermediate +

TIME
2–4 hours (preferably spaced out over more than one session)

MATERIALS
None

NUMBERS
Multiples of 3 groups each of about 3 students

LISTEN TO OUR MEETING

In this activity students prepare and carry out meetings, and provide questions for onlookers to answer. It is particularly useful for Business English classes. There are variations for other types of classes at the end.

Procedure

1 Divide the class into groups of about three students who have similar interests or job activities. If there are only three students in your class each will be working on their own. The groups don't have to be exactly the same size but there must be multiples of three groups.

2 Tell the class that each group is going to set up a meeting or discussion with one of the other groups. They must think of a situation at work where they would be having a meeting in English.

3 They write an agenda for the meeting to cover the points they want to discuss and/or the information they want to find out. If appropriate, they allocate roles.

4 They must also write down all the information the other group will need in order to participate as realistically as possible, e.g. if in a business context, they need to give the company description, job profiles, background to the meeting, any constraints or problems, etc. If in a more general context, they need to give descriptions of the people involved, the place, etc.

5 Finally, they write some listening comprehension questions to be answered by a third group, in other words, a group which isn't participating in the meeting. These should include questions which ask both for specific explicit information and also for opinions and deductions. It's also worth telling them that the order of these questions does not have to correspond with the order on their 'agenda'.

6 You check their 'agendas', information sheets, and their comprehension questions for accuracy and clarity.

7 Label the groups A, B, and C.

8 The first meeting. Group A have their meeting with group B. Group C listen and write the answers to the questions group A have given them. It is important to allow time for groups B and C to read and

assimilate the information before the meeting takes place. During the meeting group C do not actively participate.

9 After the meeting, group C give the answers to the questions. Those questions relating to their opinions naturally lead to an interesting discussion phase in which everybody can be involved.

10 Group B have their meeting with group C while group A answer the questions.

11 Group C have their meeting with group A while group B answer the questions.

NOTES

a I find that it is too draining to have all three meetings in quick succession. It works better if it is extended over a number of sessions or interspersed with other activities.

b The preparation phase could be done as homework if your students have the possibility of working together outside the classroom.

VARIATIONS

1 This technique can also be used to work on Social English in a particular setting, e.g.:
- a party
- interview with insurance company after an accident
- a family reunion
- a job interview
- a newspaper reporter
- interview with a bank manager
- buying a house
- buying/renting a car
- planning a trip

2 **Teacher training application** This activity can be used as a discussion technique. Groups can choose an aspect of teaching or learning they would like to discuss and prepare information sheets and questions for it. Group C could be given extra observational tasks, e.g. the ways people listen, sit, move their bodies, their facial expressions, how they interrupt, how they get an important point across, who is most convincing and why.

5.2

LEVEL
Elementary +

TIME
45 minutes

MATERIALS
None

NUMBERS
Minimum 12, no
maximum

NEIGHBOURS

Procedure

1 Divide the class into roughly equal-sized groups of at least four, preferably five, per group.
2 Each group forms itself into a family, or a group of relations living together. The household doesn't necessarily have to consist of a mother, father and children. Tell them all the families live on the same street. Give the groups time to decide who they are, their personalities, interests, feelings and attitudes towards the other people in their home.
3 Each group takes a turn at 'being' their family while the other groups watch.
4 At this point you could ask the other groups to describe the family they have just seen.
5 Tell the class that the next-door family in the house on their left have just moved in, and two of their family are going to visit them to welcome them. So two from each group go round to the next group on their left. They then play the visits simultaneously.
6 The visitors return to their own families and tell each other about the new people they have met.

FOLLOW-ONS

These are wide open depending on the level of the students, and the kind of families, personalities, problems, etc. which emerge from the original role plays. Possible situations could be a street party, a street meeting about a possible building development, a wedding or a business deal. Particular functions could be focused on, such as apologising, inviting, refusing, complaining, explaining or making requests.

NOTES

a This activity is fun and relaxed. Students tend to take on their chosen roles enthusiastically and confidently. Most groups seem to have one 'eccentric' in their household and at least one 'conflict' situation.
b I sometimes lead in to this activity by brainstorming some appropriate language. Alternatively I use it to practise such language. Possible areas: feelings, describing appearances, describing personalities, attitudes, interests, likes and dislikes, daily routines.

ACKNOWLEDGEMENT
I was introduced to this activity by Cynthia Beresford.

ASK ME MY QUESTIONS

This technique is particularly effective for groups of business people. It gives them the opportunity to talk in detail about their work. For applications to a General English course see Variation 2.

Procedure

1 Tell the class to imagine that they are going to act as business consultants. They are going to carry out a consultancy on their own departments.
2 Their first task (which could be done as homework) is to write a list of about fifteen questions that, as a consultant, they would ask. So, for example, a learner whose real job is a sales manager writes fifteen questions to ask the sales manager. These could be questions about the procedures, difficulties, customers or terms of payment.
3 Make enough photocopies of their questions for everyone in the group to have or see a copy. Alternatively get them to write them on an overhead transparency. Or use it as a student-student dictation exercise.
4 The group reads through student A's questions, commenting on and correcting structure and/or content. You help when necessary.
5 The group then become the consultants. Student A is 'her/himself' at work. The consultants ask student A her/his own questions, supplementing them when they wish with other questions that may arise.
6 Use the same procedure for the other students' questions.

The following are two sets of unedited questions written in one of my intermediate classes. The other questions were to the service, finance, and research and development departments.

Questions for the Commercial Department

1 What do you think about the organisation of your department?
2 Do you believe at present employees are few or too much?
3 Do you believe the organisation needs an automation?
4 Did you see raw material's market increased last year?
5 What are your prediction for the next year?
6 What do you think about the connection with the other department?
7 Do you have any idea how will be share the market between three major Italian Company?
8 Could you explain the future of your sales dept?
9 How is your best performance in gasoline sales in the last four years?
10 How is your deadline to buy oil?
11 How is your greenline for the quantity to buy?
12 Your supply are all linked oil term contracts?
13 How is the difference of valuation between two kinds of supplies?
14 Do you carry your supplies with your own ships?
15 How is the increase of the price for the transport costs?

5.3

LEVEL
Lower intermediate +

TIME
20 minutes per student (not necessarily in one session)

MATERIALS
None

NUMBERS
Groups of about 4

Questions for the Manufacturing Department

1 How many products do you make?
2 How do you control the quality?
3 How many people do you have?
4 What is your organisation?
5 What is the amount of the fixed cost?
6 How much do you spend for the people training?
7 What is the efficiency rate?
8 What is the reliability rate?
9 Do you employ temporary workers?
10 What is your plan?
11 Where are the bottlenecks on the line?
12 What is the energy cost?
13 What is the maintenance cost?
14 What is the amount of the product loss?
15 What is the maximum capacity of the factory?

NOTES

a This activity often works better if it is extended over a number of sessions, perhaps interspersed with other activities. On an intensive course one questionnaire per day works well. It's important that everyone has their fair share of time. In my experience the time is constructively spent.

b This is a reversal of the usual process where the teacher or the rest of the groups ask a student about their job. In this situation there are often questions which don't arise that a student would like to be asked.

c Each member of the group has the opportunity to talk about themself in a situation where the rest of the group are actively involved and have some control over the situation.

d Everyone practises asking detailed questions, both written and orally.

e There is the opportunity for people in different work areas to learn vocabulary and content of other work areas; the activity lends itself to spontaneous discussion and information sharing.

f **Application to a coursebook**   See Section 2, H.

VARIATIONS

1 **Teacher training application**   Teachers could write questions about their own teaching situations, beliefs, worries and ideas.

2 **General English application**   Ask students to write questions about one of their interests or hobbies.

   i Tell the class they are going to be explorers and to write questions about things they would like to find out about.

WHO AM I?

Procedure

5.4

LEVEL
Lower
intermediate +

TIME
45 minutes

MATERIALS
Sticky labels or paper
and pins or Sellotape

NUMBERS
Minimum 6, no
maximum

1 Put the students in pairs. Each student thinks of a famous personality (dead or alive), they know something about. They write the name on a piece of paper or label and pin it on their partner's back.
2 In pairs students take it in turns to ask each other yes/no questions to establish their identity.
3 They ask each other for more information about their character, e.g. If the character is John Kennedy a student might want to know when he was shot, who was accused of the murder, how many children he had.
4 Everyone takes on the role of their given character. They choose another partner, introduce themselves, and have a 'party' type conversation, i.e. social chitchat.
5 Put the students into groups of about five, separating the original pairs. Each person writes one topic they want to be interviewed about as their character, e.g. John Kennedy might choose to be interviewed about Ronald Reagan's presidency.
6 In their groups they take it in turns to be interviewed.
7 They give their labels to another student in their group to add a slogan, e.g. for John Kennedy it could be 'United We Stand'. These can be put on the wall.

FOLLOW-ONS

a Brainstorming adjectives to describe the different people.
b Brainstorming particular vocabulary or expressions they would expect the different characters to use.
c A cocktail party with all the characters 'in role'.
d Some of the characters in a train compartment.

ACKNOWLEDGEMENT
This activity sequence was compiled by Roger Woodham.

STUDENT-GENERATED ROLE PLAYS

Procedure

5.5

LEVEL
Lower
intermediate +

TIME
1 hour

MATERIALS
None

NUMBERS
Group(s) of about 4

1 Brainstorm from the class some situations or language points that they need or would like to practise.
2 Ask each person to devise and write down a scenario for one of the situations or language points. This should include full details of the people involved, their backgrounds, personalities, attitudes, objectives, etc. The creator of the role play takes a key role in it and allocates the other roles to the students in their group. It doesn't matter if there aren't enough roles to go round – the students not

actively involved can be the audience. For example, a particular situation could be 'shopping', and the characters could be:

a a sales assistant in a shoe shop.

b a customer buying a pair of shoes.

c a customer who is tired of waiting and wants to return a pair of shoes they aren't satisfied with.

d the shop manager. Very polite but not very helpful.

Give everyone time to prepare. At this point you may want to suggest or elicit the language or vocabulary they might need to do the role play. Alternatively the students could make a mind map of useful language for their situation. Other members of the group could add to it. (see Fig. 6).

They do the role plays within their groups.

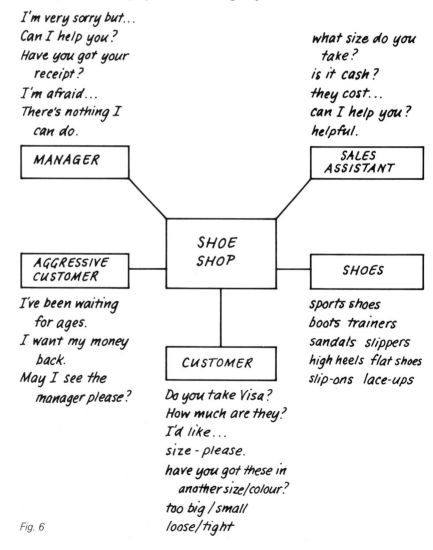

I'm very sorry but...
Can I help you?
Have you got your
   receipt?
I'm afraid...
There's nothing I
can do.

what size do you
   take?
is it cash?
they cost...
can I help you?
helpful.

MANAGER

SALES ASSISTANT

AGGRESSIVE CUSTOMER

SHOE SHOP

SHOES

I've been waiting
   for ages.
I want my money
   back.
May I see the
   manager please?

CUSTOMER

sports shoes
boots trainers
sandals slippers
high heels flat shoes
slip-ons lace-ups

Do you take Visa?
How much are they?
I'd like...
size - please.
have you got these in
   another size/colour?
too big / small
loose/tight

Fig. 6

FOLLOW-ONS

Writing dialogues, reports, jumbled conversations, one-sided dialogues, follow-up telephone calls or personality profiles.

NOTES

a In most classroom role plays students are given situations and roles by the teacher. These may or may not be situations or roles they feel comfortable in. If another student provides the framework, they will feel more free to query it and if necessary change it. The creator of the role play also has the opportunity to devise exactly what suits them.

b The process of explaining and describing the details of the roles is a difficult and valuable activity in itself.

VARIATIONS

1 Business application This technique is especially effective for learners of Business English who have particular work situations they need to carry out in English. In this case they would play 'themselves' and allocate the other parts to other students.

2 Teacher training application This is a good way for teachers to practise devising and preparing role plays, and to experience what it is like to do them.

FROM MUSIC TO STORIES
Procedure

1 Put the sheets of paper and pens round the edge of a table, or round the room on chairs. Each student stands by a piece of paper.

2 Play music and ask the students to start drawing anything that springs to their minds. Give them a couple of minutes.

3 Everyone moves round one place, taking their pen with them, and adds something to the sheet of paper now in front of them. (This means that the pictures end up multi-coloured and people can identify their own contributions).

4 Repeat Stages 2 and 3 as often as seems appropriate. In smaller groups it's possible for everyone to contribute to every picture.

5 Play the music and let everyone walk round the room looking at the finished pictures. Then let the students pick up the picture they like best.

6 Form the students into groups of about four. They pool their pictures and make up a story based on these. This is done orally but they can make a few notes if necessary to help them remember the story. At this point you can be available to help with any vocabulary, etc.

7 Each group selects a story teller who moves round to the next group

5.6

LEVEL
Lower intermediate +

TIME
45 minutes

MATERIALS
Cassette player and music cassettes, one sheet of paper per person, a different colour pen per person

NUMBERS
Minimum 8, no maximum

with the pictures and tells the story. This stage can be repeated as often as you like.

8 The story teller gives the pictures to a member of another group and entrusts that person to retell their group's story to either another group or the originators of the story.

FOLLOW-ONS

a The groups can write their stories (or a story they have been told). These are displayed and another group matches them to the pictures.

b The stories are written and cut up for another group to order.

c Two or three groups write, cut up and jumble their stories for other groups to resort and order.

d The group retell their stories with differences for the others to spot.

e The groups write their stories as mutual dictations (see Activity 3.2).

f Groups choose one of the stories they have heard to act out or mime. If it is mimed, the other groups have to guess which pictures it is based on. Alternatively groups choose a new combination of pictures to mime and the groups have to put the pictures in the right order.

g Groups use the stories to write cloze, multiple-choice or C tests (see Activity 10.8).

h Students dictate their stories and stop at the appropriate points for the others to write the dialogue.

ACKNOWLEDGEMENT
Rod Bolitho introduced me to the initial activity. He learnt it from Anne Pechou.

5.7

LEVEL
Lower intermediate +

TIME
15 minutes

MATERIALS
Chairs

NUMBERS
Group(s) of about 8

MIMING/DUBBING

Procedure

1 In large classes, form the students into groups of about eight. Ask one student in each group to arrange some chairs in any position they like such as in a circle, in rows, in front of each other, opposite each other or back to back. The number of chairs will depend on the number of students in their group because there must be at least two students per chair.

2 Ask some students in the same group to sit on them. It doesn't matter if some chairs are left empty.

3 Give the students sitting on the chairs time to decide where they are, e.g. a waiting room, a plane, an interview. They share ideas and then choose the one they like best and tell the others in their group.

4 Give them more time to decide who they are are, e.g. a bored student, a frightened patient. They tell the rest of the group.

5 Ask some other students in the same group to pair off with a sitting student.

6 Tell them they are going to be the 'voice' of the sitting partner, so they need to stand where they can see their partner's face without stopping the students on the chairs seeing each other, i.e. outside the group of chairs but opposite their partner (see Fig. 7).

Fig. 7

7 The students sitting down start to mime their situation, while those standing act as their voice and 'dub' the conversation.

8 Depending on numbers, any remaining students can each be responsible for writing one of the voices, i.e. student-student dictation. For example, in a group of eight who only have three students on the chairs, there will be two students not involved.

FOLLOW-ON

The text that the remaining students have written can then be worked on, improved, and perhaps be used for practising reported speech.

NOTES

a For more reticent students this provides a much more stress-free way of doing a role play as there is shared responsibility.

b Application to a coursebook See Section 2, B.

VARIATION

Business application Arrange the chairs for a meeting, a presentation, or an interview.

STUDENT-DIRECTED SITUATIONAL ROLE PLAYS

Procedure

1 Brainstorm a number of situations or functions the group need to practise, e.g. telephoning to confirm an air ticket, asking for information about hiring a car, disagreeing, comparing.

2 In groups of three let them choose one of these.

3 Each group decides on who will be the two 'actors' and who will be the director. Give them time to discuss their roles and if necessary ask you for any language help.

4 Each group acts out their situation to another group. While they do this the director whispers any instructions they like, e.g. *get angry*, *pretend you didn't hear*, *cry*, etc.

5.8

LEVEL
Lower
intermediate +

TIME
30 minutes

MATERIALS
None

NUMBERS
Groups of 3

5 Stage 4 can be repeated with other groups as often as they like. This will give you time to see them all.

FOLLOW-ONS

a One group writes an account of another group's role play, i.e. in reported speech.

b Students comment on the behaviour, attitudes and reactions of the different actors using *should(n't) have*, e.g. *he should have apologised.*

c Groups write out their dialogue and jumble it for another group to re-sort.

d Groups write out a one-sided version of their dialogue for another group to fill in, or use as a mutual dictation.

e One group mimes their role play and another group dubs it.

NOTE

This simple extension of a role play activity works well. Usually students are given a situation and given their role and then do the role/play – either in front of the whole class or to another group. It's easy to feel rather foolish in this situation, particularly if you have been asked to role play a part 'outside' your normal being. For example, how many of our students need to practise being a travel agent? However, if a group has picked on a situation, has been responsible for allocating roles, and also has a director to give them ideas and direction, the feeling of 'why am I doing this?' seems to evaporate.

ACKNOWLEDGEMENT

I learnt the idea of having a student 'director' from Mike Gradwell.

5.9

LEVEL
Intermediate +

TIME
10 minutes each round

MATERIALS
None

NUMBERS
Minimum 4, no maximum

WHO OR WHAT ARE YOU?

Procedure

1 Student A leaves the room and is told that when they come back they have to guess who or what they are by watching and joining in whatever the other students are doing.

2 The others decide on who or what the person is (e.g. a builder or a football) and then improvise the situation.

3 Student A comes back into the room and joins in, taking their cue from the others. For example if they are meant to be a football they may find themselves being picked up and thrown around! If they are a builder someone may ask them for advice or give them a hammer.

FOLLOW-ON

Brainstorm other vocabulary and collocations related to the person or object.

CHAPTER 6

Sentence building

This chapter focuses on stringing words together. Many students tell me they find this difficult.

SILENT WAY SENTENCES

This activity can be used to focus on a particular subject of importance to the group, or to focus on a particular structure.

Procedure

1 Ask the class to select a topic such as music, sport or cinema.
2 Ask for one or two 'secretaries' to write on the board.
3 The class call out words relevant to the topic, and the secretaries write them all over the board, not in a vertical list. It's important to have a mix of nouns, verbs, adjectives, etc.
4 These words are now used as the basis for sentences. Tell the students they are going to work individually or in pairs (depending on the size of the group) to think of a sentence which incorporates 3–5 of these words. They can add any words they want. They can also change the form of the words in their sentences, so *credible* could become *incredible,* or *power* could become *powerful.* You may want to stipulate sentences of a particular structure – depending on your reason for using the activity.
5 Start by giving an example yourself. Think of a sentence which incorporates 3–5 of the words on the board. Point to the words in your sentence in the order in which you want them. Everyone writes down a sentence incorporating these words *in that order.* Ask them to read out their sentences so that you can check they have understood the task.
6 A student or pair of students points to their words. When everyone has thought of and written down their sentences the process is repeated. I find it best to delay comparing the sentences until the end of the activity so that the concentration is not too broken.
7 At the end of the activity, when everyone has had a chance to initiate a sentence, all the alternative sentences are read out. I use this as a student-student dictation phase to encourage them to be involved in any correction process and to have a record to keep.

VARIATIONS

1 I have also used this technique to lead into a text. I give them the title

6.1

LEVEL
Elementary +

TIME
45 minutes

MATERIALS
None

NUMBERS
Any

or subject of the text we are about to read and we use that as the starting topic.

2 It can also be used as a revision activity. You can keep changing the structure, e.g. the first two sentences in the past, the next two in future conditionals, then two questions, etc.

ACKNOWLEDGEMENT

This activity is inspired by the Silent Way tradition. A variation of it is in *Dictation* (Davis and Rinvolucri 1988).

6.2

LEVEL
Elementary +

TIME
15 minutes

MATERIALS
None

NUMBERS
Group(s) of about 8

WORD CHAIN SENTENCES

Procedure

1 Each group chooses their secretary.

2 Explain that they are going to make a number of sentences which should follow on from each other. These sentences are produced by each person in turn saying a word, which is written down by the secretary. The person on the left of the secretary starts with any word, followed by the person on their left, and so on round the circle. The sentences must be grammatically correct and coherent.

3 If any student wants their word to end a sentence they must say the full stop. Then the next student starts a new sentence which must follow on logically from the previous one.

4 The secretary can be asked to read back all or any of the sentence(s) at any time.

5 Anyone can question a word if they think it does not fit for any reason.

FOLLOW-ONS

a They jumble their sentences for another group to reorder and perhaps fill in suitable linkers.

b They jumble the words of each sentence for another group to reorder.

c They omit the beginning, middle or end of one sentence for another group to write.

d They omit the beginning, middle or end of their group of sentences for another group to write.

e They change the time, e.g. from the present into the past.

f They replace some of the verbs with phrasals.

g They add three words to each sentence.

h They make the sentences more formal/informal.

i They put the sentences into direct speech.

NOTES

a If you prefer, a topic could be agreed on beforehand. In this case the activity might also be used to practise a certain area of vocabulary.

b This activity works well because it forces everyone to listen to each other.

c It is good for a mixed ability group because everyone has equal power and importance, and at the same time an opportunity to help or be helped.

VARIATIONS

Teacher training applications

1 Ask the teachers to devise the follow-ons.

2 Use this procedure to describe a particular teaching technique or approach.

WORD ORDER

This activity is excellent for focusing on a particular word order or syntax problem, such as the structure of *want to* + infinitive, order of adjectives, etc.

Procedure

1 The class chooses a word order problem to focus on. Each group writes a sentence using it – preferably with the same number of words in the sentence as there are people in the groups.

2 When you have checked their sentences, they put each word on a sticky label or piece of paper to be given to another group. Each member of that group wears a word. If the number in the group is not equal to the number of words, some people must have two consecutive words or share a word.

3 The groups get themselves into a circle in the correct order to make the sentence.

4 When you have checked the sentences the groups practise saying them with the right intonation, stress and weak forms – each person saying only their word. This is quite hard but fun. It helps if the people with the weak words (e.g. *a, to, and*) put themselves in physically weak positions, e.g. outside the circle, or on their knees. Contractions can squash together.

5 Each group 'performs' their sentence. Other groups write it down.

NOTES

a The process of actually walking to the right position for your word, rather than just looking at it on paper, helps to internalise the correct word order.

b **Application to a coursebook**   See Section 2, L.

ACKNOWLEDGEMENT
The idea of people as 'words' derives from the All's Well method in *All's Well* (Dickinson, Lévêque and Sagot 1975).

6.3

LEVEL
Elementary +

TIME
20 minutes

MATERIALS
Sticky labels or paper and pins or Sellotape

NUMBERS
Groups of about 8

CHAPTER 7

Vocabulary

The first two activities in this chapter focus on expanding vocabulary and the last three aim to activate familiar vocabulary. All of these activities can be adapted for Business English classes simply by working on relevant vocabulary areas.

7.1

LEVEL
Beginner +

TIME
45 minutes

MATERIALS
None

NUMBERS
Any

DOUBLE LANGUAGE TEXTS

This activity can only be used in monolingual groups.

Procedure

1 Let each student or pair of students write down six words in their mother tongue that they would like to know in English. If you know the mother tongue, give them the English words. Otherwise use good bilingual dictionaries.
2 Ask them to write a short passage in the mother tongue incorporating these English words. These can be repeated as often as they like.
3 They read their passages aloud.
4 On another occasion they can translate more of the words in their passages and read them aloud again.

NOTES

a This activity allows them to incorporate the new and 'foreign' into their familiar and safe background so that they can retain their identity and control over the language.
b I always liked the original version of this activity but could seldom use it, as I don't know enough languages. Because of this I had to make the students prepare the material.

VARIATION

Stages 1 and 2 can be reversed. Students think of a short story in their mother tongue that they would like to tell to their group and then choose six words from it that they would like to use in English.

ACKNOWLEDGEMENT
This strategy is used for teaching primary school immigrants in the UK. In fact it's how we naturally start to use another language. This is a variation of an activity published in *Vocabulary* (Morgan and Rinvolucri 1986).

VOCABULARY SHEETS
Procedure

1 Give each student a sheet of paper and a different colour pen.
2 Brainstorm areas of vocabulary you want to work on, such as travel, cars or selling.
3 Each group choose one of these areas (it doesn't matter if more than one group choose the same area), and each person (or pair) in the group chooses a different subheading for that area. They write this at the top of their piece of paper, so if the area the group have chosen is the language of menus, the different headings could be *meat, vegetables, starters, desserts, fish*. (In fact I have come across a number of students who need this specific language in order to translate menus with foreign visitors. Words for different kinds of fish can be crucial but we don't seem to teach them.)
4 Give everyone time to write as many words as they want to on their sheet. If they don't know a word that they want, they can either look it up in a good dictionary, or ask you. Tell them to scatter the words over the page rather than put them in a vertical list.
5 Everyone passes their sheet one place round and then works on the sheet they have been given by their neighbour. They must first read all the words on it and ask whoever wrote it about any words they don't know. Then they can add any other words they can think of.
6 The process continues until they get their original sheet back.
7 They look at their sheets and ask each other about any words that have been added that they don't understand or agree with.
8 You collect in the sheets and check them for spelling and appropriacy before the next lesson.

FOLLOW-ONS

a Each student transfers their words to a mind map (see Activity 5.5 and Testing Activity 10.1f).
b Each student chooses ten words from their sheet that they want to activate and puts them into sentences.
c They categorise their words under whatever headings they choose, so for *fish* the categories could be *I like* and *I don't like* and *OK*.
d The sheets are put on the wall.

NOTES

a The point of everyone having a different colour pen is that it is then easier for people to identify who wrote a word they need to ask about.
b **Application to a coursebook**   See Section 2, F.

VARIATION

Teacher training application   The categories could be teaching methods, approaches, areas or how to teach the different skills, etc.

7.2

LEVEL
Elementary +

TIME
30 minutes

MATERIALS
Sheets of paper and different colour pens

NUMBERS
Group(s) of 4–6

ACKNOWLEDGEMENT
For the original idea see the article 'Classroom Dictionary' in *Modern English Teacher* (Woodward 1988).

7.3

LEVEL
Lower
intermediate +

TIME
30 minutes

MATERIALS
None

NUMBERS
Group(s) of about 8

STUDENT DEFINITIONS

Procedure

1 Choose an area or category of vocabulary you want to work on.
2 Ask each student to think of a word in the chosen area of vocabulary.
3 They write it on a piece of paper and give it to you to check and keep.
4 They each write a definition of their word on a clean piece of paper. This should be as clear and unambiguous as possible and it must not contain the word, so they use X instead of the word itself.
5 When you have checked their definition, they put it on a table for everyone to see.
6 Deal out the pieces of paper with the original words on, making sure no one gets their own word. Everyone stands up and mills round the table.
7 They match the word they have been dealt with its definition.

FOLLOW-ONS

a The words are incorporated into an article, story or dialogue.
b Write the other forms of the word, e.g. the adjective of the noun.

NOTES

a Take vocabulary from a text they have been or are going to be working on.
b It doesn't matter if more than one person chooses the same word. It is interesting for them to see the different definitions.

VARIATION

Teacher training application For pre-service training use EFL jargon, grammatical labels, and terms for different teaching approaches

ACKNOWLEDGEMENT
This is a variation of an idea from *Vocabulary* (Morgan and Rinvolucri 1986).

SPOT THE SIMILAR WORD
Procedure

1 The class brainstorm onto the board the new words they have come across recently. Allow them to refer to their notes for these. They can include words heard out of class – particularly if you have encouraged them to keep a record of these.
2 Students now work individually, in pairs or in small groups. Tell each person or group to select about six of the words on the board that they want to use, and to put them into a passage, such as a story, letter or set of instructions. You check these for appropriate usage of the words and grammatical accuracy.
3 They rewrite this passage, replacing the six words with synonyms or paraphrases. You check this.
4 They write the original words on separate pieces of paper.
5 These are shared round the class.
6 Individuals or groups take it in turns to read their passage aloud.
7 The other students concentrate on the word on their paper and shout it out when they hear the synonym or paraphrase. They then make a note of that particular sentence but insert the alternative word(s) on their card.
8 Student-student dictation. The other students read out their sentences to retell the passage, which will now contain the six words that the person or group chose from the board.

ACKNOWLEDGEMENT
This activity is an extension of an idea of Lou Spaventa.

7.4
LEVEL
Lower intermediate +

TIME
45 minutes

MATERIALS
None

NUMBERS
Any even number of groups of about 4

VOCABULARY CARDS
Procedure

1 Depending on numbers, students work individually, in pairs or in small groups.
2 Ask them to choose about twenty words they have recently come across that they would like to learn and activate. Encourage them to look through their notes for these. (This is one way of making sure their notes become active and useful rather than 'freezers' to be opened on a rainy day, if at all.)
3 They then write each word on a separate card. You check their spelling.
4 They give their pile of cards to another group to look at. This group then devises or chooses a game or activity to go with these cards. They will need some guidance here, unless in previous lessons you have used cards for activities or games. Tell them to think of any card

7.5
LEVEL
Upper elementary +

TIME
45 minutes

MATERIALS
Small pieces of card or paper

NUMBERS
Group(s) of about 4

games they have played at home that could be adapted to their cards, such as Snap, Pairs (Pelmanism), Rummy or Bingo. Alternatively they think of a language activity, such as building collocations (e.g. adding an adjective to the noun cards, a noun to the verb cards, an adverb to the verb cards), categorising or incorporating some cards into sentences.

5 They write the instructions for their activity, give them to you to check, and then return the cards with the instructions to the original group, who will play the game. Here is an unedited example from an upper elementary group.

Pelmanism/Pairs   Put the cards face down over the table. Objective – to make the most pairs. A pair is a picture with the right caption. The bigger cards are the pictures. Student 1 looks at one big card and one little one. If they are a pair they keep them and try again. If they aren't a pair they put them back in the same place face down on the table. Then Student 2 does the same thing.

Comment   I did help them with a few of the words, like *keep*. In fact they missed out an important instruction which had to be added later when another group tried the game, which was 'when the players choose their cards everyone else in the group must be able to see them'. After they had played their games we went back to the instructions and worked on particular vocabulary for games, like *player, deal, lay the cards* and *a turn.* They then rewrote their instructions incorporating these.

NOTES

a More often than not there is an overlap between the groups' choice of words. This has a positive and reinforcing effect.

b This activity gets over the problem of choosing an activity for students to prepare instructions for. We may ask them to give instructions for mending a bicycle puncture but there is not much chance of these instructions actually being carried out in the classroom, rather than just mimed. By having a real task we can put the instructions to a real and immediate test.

c The different piles of words can be mixed together in future classes for other activities.

VARIATIONS

1 Ask students to produce 'grammatical cards' for other groups, such as irregular verbs. They select about ten verbs and write each part (e.g. *buy, bought, bought*) on a different card.

2 **Teacher training application**   This is an excellent technique for teachers to focus on giving clear instructions. In my experience this is an art that not many of us easily master.

CHAPTER 8

Writing

Many students are frightened of writing in another language. I certainly feel the same when I try it. (In fact, it's hard enough in my own language). It's a big risk putting words on paper that may be wrong. At least if we say a mistake we don't usually have to repeat it, but words on paper can be read again and again. This chapter focuses on collaborative writing which spreads the responsibility and should reduce the risk of making mistakes.

WORDS TO SENTENCES TO PARAGRAPHS

Procedure

1 Divide the board into two columns. At the top of one column write *A* and at the top of the other write *B*. Under *A* write a positive verb and under *B* write a negative verb in the same semantic area, for example, under *A help* and under *B ignore*. These words don't have to be opposites, but one should have a positive feel, and the other a negative feel.

2 Ask the class to add at least eleven more pairs, which they dictate to a 'secretary' to write on the board.

3 Get them to select six *A* verbs from the board and write them all on a piece of paper, adding to each one a noun that collocates with it.

4 Then ask them to do the same on another piece of paper with the *B* verbs.

5 Put the papers into an *A* pile and a *B* pile. Each student chooses one piece of paper (containing six verbs plus collocation) from each pile.

6 Distribute pieces of A4 paper and show them how to fold them into eight with good creases for tearing, as shown in Fig. 8.

7 From their papers they select four *A* verbs and nouns and four *B* verbs and nouns. They put these into eight sentences, writing them on the creased A4 paper. The

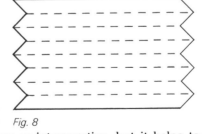

Fig. 8

sentences can be simple, complex or interrogative, but it helps to suggest which tense the students should use.

8 Students then tear the paper into eight strips.

9 Form the students into groups of three. In their groups they pool their sentences and choose between the *A*s and the *B*s. They then try

8.1

LEVEL
Intermediate +

TIME
1 hour

MATERIALS
Pieces of A4 paper

NUMBERS
Minimum 3, no maximum

to sequence as many of them as possible that will fit logically and coherently together to form a paragraph.

10 Individually, the students then write a more polished version of their group's paragraph. At this point they can omit or add ideas, connectors, etc. There will then be three similar, but not identical versions, of the same paragraph. This stage could be done as homework.

ACKNOWLEDGEMENT
I first saw this activity used by Roger Woodham in Poland.

8.2

LEVEL
Lower
intermediate +

TIME
45 minutes

MATERIALS
None

NUMBERS
Group(s) of about 4

STUDENT-STUDENT REFERENCES

Procedure

1 Decide on a job or profession that the class would like to think about. Brainstorm the job activities and any relevant vocabulary.

2 Divide the class into an even number of groups of about four.

3 Tell them that each person is going to write a reference to help a member of another group to get this particular job, for example, group A write references for the people in group B and vice versa, group C with group D, etc. In their groups students decide who will write whose reference. Tell them not to give the name of the student they are writing the reference for. The objective is to make their reference as clear as possible so that the other group will easily be able to recognise who it applies to.

4 Within their groups they check each other's writing and ask you for any help.

5 The groups get together and read out their references. The other group has to guess which of them it applies to.

NOTES

a One group I did this with chose the job of a teacher. I decided they would all have made very good ones!

b This is a very useful activity for Business English classes.

FOLLOW-ONS

a Job interviews.
b Letters of application.
c Job descriptions.
d Personality profiles.

JOINT STORY WRITING

The first time you use this activity you should provide the story so that your students can have a model.

Procedure

Choose or make up a short story or anecdote. At appropriate points interrupt it with a question or task, so that what you are giving is a framework for your students to elaborate on, for example:

In Piccadilly there is a very popular pub.
Describe it.
Last time I was there a girl put some money in the juke box.
What music did she choose?

The students write down their responses. Make it clear that you want them to write whole sentences, not just words.

STUDENT-GENERATED VERSIONS
1 Individually, in pairs or small groups, the students prepare a story to tell the rest of the class. At certain points in the narrative they give instructions for other students to carry out, in other words they provide a framework from which the rest of the class can write their own stories.
2 You check and work on their stories with them before they dictate them. This is an important input stage where you can give them alternative vocabulary and check there are no mistakes.
3 When you have gone through their stories with them, the students read them out and pause at the appropriate points for the others to carry out the instructions, and write down their responses. Alternatively the story can be written up on the board, photocopied or put on an overhead transparency. In larger classes put two groups together to work on each other's stories.
4 Students compare their different versions. The following is an unedited example from an Italian student:

It is a frozen night when a sudden light sparkles everything around the oak wood. It is a mushroom-shaped astroship, it is going to inspect and take some photos of the earth. A little girl, very curious, looking outside of her window falls down from that strange luminous object. The astroship can't stop there any longer and has to keep on its journey. The little girl soon after her fallen comes to. She has only one apparent difference from human beings: two antennas like two springs over her head.

Describe the emotions and feelings of the little girl when she finds herself in this strange unknown world/planet.

She is tired and so she decides to sleep at the feet of one of this wonderful big trees. In the morning strange sounds, like children's voices awake her up.

LEVEL
Intermediate +

TIME
45 minutes

MATERIALS
None

NUMBERS
Minimum 2, no maximum

Describe the meet with these children, and what they do all together.

She is hungry. It is nine hours from her last dinner and she has no pills with her. She can't speak or understand the children's language but they understand what she wants and decide to take her in their house, but there are some problems.

Describe the problems and the way they solve them.

After a year suddenly the same light and noise sparkles the same wood. She can feel the presence of the astroship with her antennas.

Try to finish the history
p.s. If you want you can insert; 'describe the little girl' at the beginning.

This had to be edited, e.g.

It was a dark freezing night in the oak forest. Suddenly everywhere was bathed in sparkling light. A mushroom-shaped spaceship approached nearer and nearer. Leaning out of one of its port-holes a little girl fell out and down to earth. She was a curious creature with two antennae protruding from her head.

Describe the little girl

The little girl had been stunned by her fall but now she came to. She looked around this strange world she had landed on. It was still half dark with daylight filtering in from the East.

Describe her feelings

ACKNOWLEDGEMENT
This idea is an adaptation of a technique where the teacher provides the skeleton in *Once Upon A Time* (Morgan and Rinvolucri 1983).

8.4 WRITING DIALOGUES

LEVEL
Elementary +

Dialogues written by students can be used for many different purposes, such as practising intonation, pronunciation, register, dictations, role plays, reordering, expanding, summarising, indirect speech. The dialogues can be generated in a number of different ways:

a Students write six keywords (e.g. new words they have come across recently), and give them to (an)other student(s) to incorporate into a dialogue.
   Application to a coursebook See Section 2, E.
b Students write the last line of a dialogue and give it to (an)other student(s) to write the dialogue and read out.

c Students write the beginning and ending of a dialogue and give it to (an)other student(s) to add the middle.

d Students give each other a dialogue in a formal register to be put into an informal register.

e Students give each other about eight exchanges to order into a cohesive dialogue. At higher levels they can be encouraged to make them quite open so there is more than one possibility for the order.

e.g. *Perhaps.* *So what will happen?*
    I don't know. *Is it?*
    What do you think? *It's obvious.*
    Was it really his fault?

They then act them out for the other groups to decide on the situation and background.

f   **i** Ask each student to bring an object into class, e.g. a scarf, ornament or kitchen knife.

  ii They exchange objects with another student.

  iii Put the class into pairs and tell them that each object represents a person, and they must decide on who that person is, i.e. their character, job, status, way of life. This can be an actual or a fictitious person. (In one of my classes, a student was given a china dog which reminded her of her grandmother who had had a similar object, so her person was her grandmother.)

  iv The students tell their partner who they are and then decide on a situation where these two people are together.

  v They write the dialogue. It's a good idea to encourage them to improvise it before they write it.

g Students bring in pictures of people talking and display them round the room or on a table. Pairs choose a picture and write the dialogue. The others have to guess which picture they chose.

NOTE

It is important that you help and check the students' finished work with them before they share it with each other.

CHAPTER 9

Error correcting

These activities force students to focus on the mistakes they keep making, usually out of sheer habit. They are fossilising deep-seated errors which are the most difficult to lose. This isn't surprising because our students have probably been practising these errors for a long time!

9.1

LEVEL
Beginner +

TIME
30 minutes

MATERIALS
None

NUMBERS
Any

STUDENT MISTAKE JINGLES
Procedure

1 Put the class into groups of students who share the same mistake.
2 As a group ask them to write a jingle with many examples of the problem in its correct form. This can be written on a big sheet of paper, OHP transparency, or flip chart so that it can be shown to the whole class.
3 Groups perform their jingles.
  The following examples came from an upper intermediate group of business people in Germany. I have chosen examples from a high level group, as in my experience it is at this level that such mistakes are the hardest to eradicate. I often find it difficult to identify in what 'surroundings' students make a particular mistake. Their jingles can often identify this for me and for them. These are the original jingles which emerged, including the mistakes, which the group finally identified for themselves.

1 'Information(s)'

I lived in a nation
With lots of information
Reading information all my life.
I had no information, had no wife,
Most of the information *were* nice
but *they* all had its special price.
But there's no information
like show information
A sum of information
With *many* information
That's like a bunch of information
In the age of information
And the moral of this information
is to kill old information
to have more animation
for further information.

2 Conditional
Sung to 'Hoochy Coochy Man' – John Lee Hooker

If your shirt isn't clean
Don't make a scene!
If you haven't a washing machine
Don't get a spleen
'Cause our team created a cream
If you put the cream on the shirt
Your eye will never be hurt
If you feel lucky then
You'll buy 'Cleany' again and again.

STRUCTURES PERPETUALLY WRONG

Procedure

1 Tell the class they are going to imagine they have all had the same dream.
2 Two students leave the room.
3 The rest of the class decide on the dream. Then together they decide on one of their mistakes they all want to focus on.
4 The two students come back and ask questions round the room to find out about the dream. The group have to answer the question using their selected structure correctly, for example, if they have chosen to work on *used to* they must use this structure in their answer:

Q: Did you like this dream?
A: I used to, but I don't any more.

5 This continues until the two students have guessed the structure and found out about the dream.

ACKNOWLEDGEMENT
Marjorie Baudains

9.2

LEVEL
Lower
intermediate +

TIME
10 minutes

MATERIALS
None

NUMBERS
Minimum 2, no
maximum

9.3

LEVEL
Elementary +

TIME
20 minutes

MATERIALS
None

NUMBERS
Any

WRONG OR RIGHT?

Procedure

1 Ask the students to write down sentences they know are wrong but that feel right to them.
2 Now ask them to do the reverse, i.e. to write sentences they know are right but which feel wrong to them.
3 They read out their sentences and explain their feelings about them.

NOTES

This gives you valuable information, and the process of talking about it helps the students to focus on various problem areas. For example, I have severe problems with the word for 'sorry' in Polish. So much so that I can't even quote it now. This is because for me it's too long and clumsy-sounding to feel apologetic. A further example is that of a friend who found it hard to accept the Portuguese word *obrigado* meaning 'thank you' beause he couldn't say it and smile at the same time!

VARIATIONS

1 Students could write sentences they know are wrong and feel wrong, or ones they know are right and feel right. This will reinforce what they already know.
2 They could write sentences they know are wrong that are regularly used by one of their peers (without mentioning any names). These can be put on the board and discussed. For example, if some people in the group regularly forget the third person 's' the student who notices this has an opportunity to point it out. This can help to relieve any frustration they might have felt at being exposed to other people's mistakes.
3 **Teacher training application** It's helpful and salutary to be reminded of these feelings. I certainly sympathise with British learners of French who want to say *je suis mangeant* for *I'm eating*.

ACKNOWLEDGEMENT
The initial sequence was devised by Paul Davis and is also in *Grammar Games* (Rinvolucri 1984).

ANOTHER NOUGHTS AND CROSSES

Procedure

1 Divide the class into an even number of teams of about four students.
2 Draw a noughts and crosses grid on the board (see Fig. 9), and explain to one student from each team how to play. One student writes an O and the other an X. The idea is to fill a vertical, horizontal or diagonal line with their letter. They take it in turns to write a letter in one of the nine squares.
3 Explain to the class that they are going to use this technique to test each other on certain language areas.
4 The class chooses the nine language areas they want to work on. Alternatively, if there are only two teams, each team could choose three and you choose the remaining three. With more teams each team chooses one area. Get them to write these areas on the grid on the board. The completed grid for intermediate students could look something like the one in Fig. 10.
5 Each team writes a testing question for each of the nine squares, e.g. for *Simple past*: *What is the past of "drink"?* and for *Apologising*: *How could you respond to "I'm sorry"?* They must also write any possible answers. Obviously the kind of questions will depend on the level of the students. The number of questions for each grid will depend on the number of rounds you want to play.
6 You must check their questions and answers before the game starts. If necessary the game can be played in a subsequent lesson.
7 Two teams play together. Team A chooses a square. A member of team B reads out their question for that square. Team A have time to confer and then give their answer. If this is accepted by team B and by you, team A can put their O in the square. If not, team B give the correct answer and put their X in the square.

NOTE

I have often used this activity at the end of a course as a round-up of the areas we have worked on.

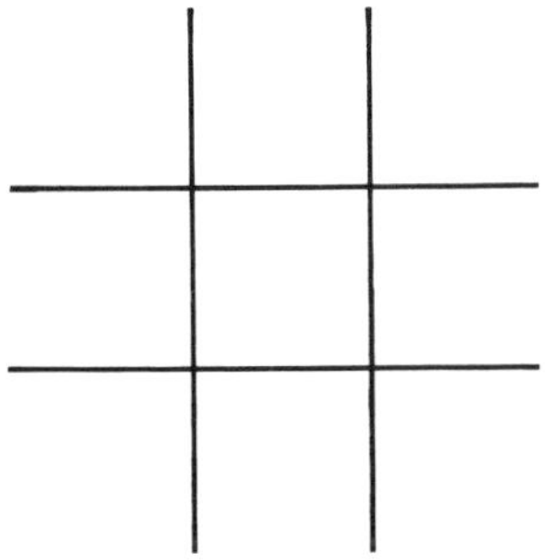

9.4

LEVEL
Beginner + (The table below would be for intermediate level)

TIME
45 minutes

MATERIALS
None

NUMBERS
Minimum 2, no maximum

Fig. 9

Simple past	since/ for	phrasal verbs
future conditionals	don't have to/ mustn't	Apologising
Prepositions of time	Parts of a car	How much/ many

Fig. 10

CHAPTER 10

Student tests

It seems to be very difficult to provide fair, effective and informative testing in language teaching. As a result I am ashamed to say I have all too often 'solved' this problem by ignoring it, i.e. by never testing. However, from the learners' point of view this is unfair. It becomes difficult for them to assess their progress, or indeed even to feel any progress, and this can lead to frustration and a feeling of inadequacy, all of which can affect motivation.

I would like to suggest some strategies to try to get over this problem. The first one I will only cover briefly, just as a reminder of familiar teacher-generated test types. The other strategies are student-generated alternatives.

10.1 TEACHER-GENERATED TESTING

Provide regular opportunities for the students to explicitly see what they have been working on and how thoroughly they have learnt it. This means regular testing of the course content, for which they can prepare by reviewing their notes. These tests do not necessarily have to be assessed but they obviously must be checked. I do these tests orally and always give them prior notice. Here are a few simple ways of doing this. I include them not because they are anything new, but as a reminder that we can and should regularly 'test' and it is quite easy to do so.

a Give them back their original mistakes, i.e. their wrong sentences you have made notes of and have worked on. Ask them to find the mistakes and correct them.

b Pick out recent new vocabulary and test it for pronunciation. Spell the words and ask them to underline the stressed syllable or silent letters. To test meaning, ask them to write a definition or a translation or put it in a sentence.

c Describe a situation for them to provide the language for, e.g. describe a problem for them to offer advice.

d In monolingual classes some language areas can be effectively and tangibly tested by asking them to translate from L1 to L2.

e Dictate cloze passages for them to write down the missing words. I usually focus on just one area, such as prepositions.

f For situations ask them to fill in mind maps including nouns, verbs, adjectives and expressions, such as the one in Fig. 11.

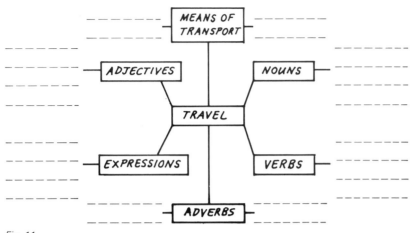

Fig. 11

10.2 STUDENT-GENERATED TESTING

1 Give the students regular opportunities to suggest the areas they want to be tested on. This should involve them looking through their books and notes, which in itself is a good revision exercise.

2 Students, individually or in groups, devise tests for each other and write answer sheets. You will have to give them examples of the kind of tests you want them to devise. When you have checked and discussed their test with them, they are exchanged round the class. When they have been completed they are returned to the authors to be marked. I think it is important that at this point they explain or justify any corrections they make to the students concerned. If they don't agree, then they must ask you to arbitrate. For examples, see Activities 10.3–10.8.

10.3 REVERSE MULTIPLE-CHOICE TESTS

The process of writing multiple-choice questions provides an opportunity for students to consolidate and think about the language. This could be a comprehension activity or it could focus on grammar or vocabulary. I think it's more interesting for them to reverse the usual procedure of writing three false answers and one true, to three true answers and one false. This means they will focus more on what is right than on what is wrong. And it is perhaps more satisfying when answering the questions to cross out a wrong answer rather than tick a right one.

This activity works well when working with long texts or perhaps ESP texts. Different groups of students can prepare questions on different sections and then exchange them. The fact that they have provided three correct answers for each question helps the rest of the group to understand the text more quickly. A text can be read or listened to.

Another appropriate piece of material is the news, with different groups writing the questions on news items.

Preparing multiple-choice questions for vocabulary is a good active process to help get new words into long-term memory. Writing three different right definitions, aspects or descriptions of a word demands a sound understanding and a lot of thinking.

The following unedited examples come from an advanced class who selected new words they had come across over the week:

A *beehive hairdo:*
1 a pony tail
2 hairstyle characteristic for the 60s
3 it's very tall
4 it takes a long time to do

B *stiletto heels:*
1 weapon used by Italians
2 shoes with very high heels
3 uncomfortable footwear
4 very elegant part of an outfit

C *nearside:*
1 for an English driver in England – the left side
2 people suffering from this defect have to wear glasses
3 a side of a car
4 opposite offside

D *receding hairline:*
1 going grey
2 bald
3 losing hair
4 less hair with age

10.4 CLOZE TESTS

Teachers spend a lot of time preparing these but this process can be a useful learning activity for students. It could be argued that preparing them is at least as useful as doing them. Depending on their level, students can either write their own from scratch, or make them from existing texts. As they white out or cross out the words, they have to make a note of them so they can check the other students' answers. It's a good idea to make the students correct the tests without their notes first and then double check them with their notes. Different groups could focus on different difficulties that they want to work on.

10.5 MATCHING EXERCISES

Students can prepare matching exercises for each other, for example, words and definitions, phrasal verbs and paraphrases, statements and responses (e.g. *I'm sorry, Don't worry*), formal and informal ways of saying the same thing, direct and indirect speech, etc. At beginner level they could work on areas such as furniture and rooms, parts of the body and clothes, etc.

10.6 COMPREHENSION TESTS

See examples in Chapter 2.

10.7 VOCABULARY TESTS

Students could prepare skeleton mind maps (see Activity 10.1) on which they leave most branches blank, for example they choose the topic and draw the rest of the map, with some branches labelled and others not. They must have a completed version themsevles.

10.8 C TESTS

Students could prepare C tests for each other. In th__ __ technique t__ __ second ha__ __ of ev__ __ __ other wo__ __ is del__ __ __ __ __ . If th__ __ __ is a th__ __ __ __ letter wo__ __ the sec__ __ __ __ two let__ __ __ __ __ are del__ __ __ __ __ . If th__ __ __ __ is a fi__ __ letter wo__ __ the sec__ __ __ __ three let__ __ __ __ __ are del__ __ __ __ __ , etc. T__ __ indefinite art__ __ __ __ __ and t__ __ word 'I' a__ __ not del__ __ __ __ __ . The fi__ __ __ sentence i__ left com__ __ __ __ __ e. More adva__ __ __ __ __ students co__ __ __ __ pre__ __ __ __ __ a pas__ __ __ __ __ on a sub__ __ __ __ __ /topic th__ __ has be__ __ included i__ the les__ __ __ __ __ and gi__ __ it t__ the tea__ __ __ __ __ to ch__ __ __ __ before crea__ __ __ __ __ the te__ __ __ . Lower lev__ __ __ __ could b__ gi__ __ __ __ the mate__ __ __ __ __ to del__ __ __ __ , thereby hav__ __ __ __ the oppor__ __ __ __ __ __ __ to re__ __ it wh__ __ __ __ they a__ __ making t__ __ test, e.g. i__ you wa__ __ them t__ fo__ __ __ __ on a parti__ __ __ __ __ __ point o__ grammar y__ __ could eit__ __ __ __ provide t__ __ text o__ get th__ __ to wr__ __ __ __ it. Ot__ __ __ __ areas t__ focus o__ could b__ particular situa__ __ __ __ __ __ , styles, ar__ __ __ __ of vocab__ __ __ __ __ , etc.

CHAPTER 11

Finishing a course

Probably the worst way to finish a course is with a test. This doesn't mean that we shouldn't give an end-of-course test, but that it should be followed by activities which reflect on what has been happening in our classes. I'd rather my students left me in the role of a helper and encourager than as an assessor. However, 90 per cent of the courses I have been on as a student have ended with a test, and no opportunity to 'round off' my involvement with the course, the teacher, or the group.

11.1

LEVEL
Elementary +

TIME
45 minutes

MATERIALS
None

NUMBERS
Minimum 6, no maximum

STUDENT-GENERATED COURSE FEEDBACK
Procedure

1 Ask everyone individually to write one question that they would like to answer on a course feedback questionnaire.
2 Divide the class into groups of 6–12.
3 Distribute A4 sheets of paper.
4 In their groups the students dictate their questions to the rest of the group who write them on their piece of paper, leaving a space between each for their answers later. It's important to establish that all questions are valid and that they must not criticise or query anyone else's contribution.
5 At this point you can dictate a question that is important to you if you want to.
6 Give the students time to write their answers individually and then collect them in.

NOTE

This idea came to me at the end of a British Council teacher training course in Poland, and it came to me as a direct result of panic. The last day of this particular course coincided with the Pope's visit to this town which meant that the majority of the participants wanted to leave early – before we had devised a feedback questionnaire. (The Pope in Poland is unfair competition!) Since this occasion I have never bothered to write one. The questions offered were more informative than the answers, and certainly more pertinent than my questions could have been.

The following is the questionnaire which emerged on this occasion. The second example is from intermediate students after a five day intensive residential course.

Example 1 Unedited, from teachers.

1 How did the course help you to improve your way of teaching?
2 What thing we have done together do you find most valuable?
3 Would you like to have sessions in which particular participants take the role of a teacher?
4 Do you think that we missed something rather important while insisting on other things that were of great interest to us?
5 Are four days enough for a course like this or would you like it to last longer? If so, how much longer?
6 Has the course helped you to have a closer look at yourself as a teacher and how does it affect you?
7 What activities we have done here won't you apply in your teaching and why?
8 How did you feel at the end of each day? Choose the answer or give your own. a) tired b) satisfied c) indifferent d) exhausted but happy.
9 Which things we discussed during the course are you going to apply to your teaching?
10 Would a follow-up session be necessary and useful?
11 How would you account for the participants gaining motivation and involvement obviously emerging from the attitude of all of us?
12 What's the most important insight you've gained from the course?

Example 2 Unedited, from language learners.

1 Do you think the kind of teaching helps you to make progress?
2 Have the activities had a positive reaction to motivate you?
3 Do you like the games, and if so, do you think you learn better by this way?
4 Do you think that you could better phone or discuss than at the beginning of the seminar?
5 Did you like the games you played at night?
6 Did you want to do more activities like student-generated stories?
7 Would you like to do more grammar studies?
8 Did you enjoy the seminar?
9 Were grammar problems solved?
10 Did you learn phrases, vocabulary for your own work?

11.2

LEVEL
Elementary +

TIME
30 minutes

MATERIALS
None

NUMBERS
Any

LETTERS TO THE NEXT GROUP
Procedure

At the end of a course ask each participant to write a letter to a member of your next group. If you have the names of this group you give each person a name to write to. Tell the students to welcome the new course members and to give them any information or advice they think they would find useful.

FOLLOW-ON

Get the group to help you to collate the information in their letters under different headings. This will probably lead to a natural and useful discussion about the course and will provide you with useful feedback to apply to your next group.

Some possible headings for a language course:

Timetable, materials, activities, problems, warnings, things that were easy, things that were difficult, things that were fun, things that were boring.

On a teacher training course they might include:

Language improvement, methodology, timetable, useful tips, useful activities, unuseful activities.

NOTE

I know teachers who write personal letters to students about to start on one of their courses. This must have a positive effect on a new student who will naturally be feeling apprehensive or curious. Receiving a letter from someone who has already been on a similar course could be very reassuring and help to break the ice. Of course, there may be some letters which could have the reverse effect! These will serve more as feedback for our own use than as a welcome for the newcomers.

11.3

LEVEL
Elementary +

TIME
30 minutes

MATERIALS
None

NUMBERS
Any

RESOLUTIONS
Procedure

1 Ask the group to get into pairs with someone they think they will be keeping in touch with after the course. If there are odd numbers you can be in a pair, or there could be a group of three.
2 Each person writes a resolution for their learning or teaching for the next six months. An opening line could be *I, (name) promise (name of partner) that by the end of the next six months I will have . . . .*
3 They exchange these contracts with their partners.
4 Everyone is responsible for contacting their partner on the relevant date to establish whether or not the resolution has been carried out.
5 If the group want to, they can show each other their resolutions and explain why they made them.

NOTE

On the course where I used this idea, one of the pairs insisted on signing their contracts in blood. Unfortunately I never discovered if this gesture made them more or less determined to keep their resolutions.

WHAT I REMEMBER ABOUT YOU IS ...

Procedure

1 Get the class to pin or stick paper on each others' backs.
2 The class mingles and writes a comment on the papers. These comments should be something positive that they associate with that person, such as 'your simulation of an angry train passenger', 'your smile' or 'your purple shoes'.

NOTE

It's up to you whether or not you want to take part in this activity, but I, along with my students, appreciate having this memento of a course, and it's not very often in life that we can be sure that people will say only nice things about us!

ACKNOWLEDGEMENT
I first learned this activity from Satish Patel.

11.4

LEVEL
Elementary +

TIME
20 minutes

MATERIALS
Pieces of paper, about size A4 and pins or Sellotape

NUMBERS
Minimum 4, no maximum

GIVING PRESENTS

Procedure

1 This activity needs to be set up a few days before the end of a course.
2 Tell the group that they are going to give each member of the group a present that they think will be particularly suitable for that person. There are two ways of doing this:
   a The group may choose a price limit per present and actually buy the presents.
   b They can just write on pieces of paper the present they would buy and perhaps the reason for their choice.
3 On the last day of the course the presents are exchanged and perhaps displayed.

ACKNOWLEDGEMENT
I am not absolutely sure where I first came across this idea, but I do know that I have heard John Morgan and Mike Gradwell talk about it.

11.5

LEVEL
Elementary +

TIME
30 minutes (depending on numbers)

MATERIALS
Possibly money!

NUMBERS
Group(s) of about 6

11.6 CLASS FOLDERS

This would be an on-going activity throughout a course. I have put it in this section only because it would not be completed before the end of the course.

Procedure

1 At the beginning of a course explain that you want the group to produce a written record of the course activities. In practice this will mean that for each lesson two people will be responsible for writing up what happened. It is important that this is done before the next session or day and given to you to check.

2 This summary, introduced by the students who wrote it, can be used as a starting point each day – to think back over the previous day, a chance for people to verbalise any worries or questions they have, and a chance to review.

3 If you have wall space, the original can be put on the wall for regular reference. If you have photocopying facilities, each member of the group can have a copy for their folder.

4 There are many other things that can be added to the folder by the end of the course, such as a class address list, photographs, resolutions, letters from each other, jokes, cards or class biographies.

Bibliography

Abbs, B and Freeman, I 1982 *Opening Strategies* Longman

Cooper, R, Maley, A and Rinvolucri, M 1989 *Video* OUP

Curran, C 1972 *Counselling Learning: A Whole Person Model For Education* Apple River Press

Davis, P and Rinvolucri, M 1988 *Dictation* CUP

Deller, S 1986 *Practical English Teaching* (**7**) 1

Dickson, Lévêque and Sagot 1975 *All's Well* Didier

Gattegno, C 1976 *Common Sense in Language Teaching* Educational Solutions, New York

Graham, C 1978 *Jazz Chants* OUP

Klippel, F 1985 *Keep Talking* CUP

Morgan, J and Rinvolucri, M 1983 *Once Upon A Time* CUP

Morgan J, and Rinvolucri, M 1986 *Vocabulary* OUP

Rinvolucri, M 1984 *Grammar Games* CUP

Stevick, EW 1980 *Teaching Languages: A Way and Ways* Newbury House

Woodward, T 1988 Classroom Dictionary *Modern English Teacher* (**15**) 3 Spring p31

Woodward, T 1988 *Loop Input* Pilgrims Publications (soon to be published as *Models and Metaphors in Language Teacher Training* CUP)